# 12 STEPS TO SUCCESS:

## BECOME THE AMAZING ADULT THE UNIVERSE WANTS YOU TO BE

**TODD KILPATRICK**

Produced by:

# FriesenPress

Suite 300 – 852 Fort Street

Victoria, BC, Canada V8W 1H8

www.friesenpress.com

Distributed to the trade by The Ingram Book Company

# Table of Contents

# INTRODUCTION

Perhaps the hardest part about being young is realizing how much time and hard work it takes to be successful when you want everything now. The marketers tell you that you need it today and a lot of us believe them. Add to that the illusion of shortcuts tempting you to make poor decisions, and life can get frustrating. Fortunately, there are real answers available. Those who think long term, give to others, take responsibility for their life and work hard find great satisfaction. You wouldn't want it any other way. You wouldn't want a world where someone does next to nothing and it all comes easily. It wouldn't be fair. Energy out has to equal energy back or the world wouldn't make sense. Those who are kind to others get kindness back. Those who are unkind to others are avoided or get into trouble with the law.

Following these 12 steps will give you a framework to live by. You can expect amazing success with health, wealth and relationships. Focus on positive decisions and behaviour, and then dare to dream.

# STEP 1:
## BE A GIVER

*I must be willing to give whatever it takes to do good to others. This requires that I be willing to give until it hurts. Otherwise, there is no true love in me, and I bring injustice, not peace, to those around me.*
—Mother Teresa

Be a giver and not a taker. Giving to others and the community creates an energy that comes straight back to you. Those who give more than they take are much more successful, and for good reason. You want to help those who are generous and you want to stay away from and maybe even hinder those who are takers.

If you know anyone with a kind, giving heart, you will go out of your way to help her. If she has a store you may buy from her. If she works for you, you want to give her raises to stay with you. You will go out of your way for kind and giving people, befriending them and speaking highly of them. You'll probably do the opposite for unkind people.

No one wants to be around those who are self-centred. You don't want to work with them, deal with them or live near them. They are narcissistic and think the rules of the universe apply to everyone but themselves. They may lie and cheat to make themselves look good. They may have some short-term success in their endeavours if they have a forceful personality. They may have some sales achievements and may even sneak up the success ladder, but eventually they will have difficulty with relationships, work and with themselves.

At the extreme end of the spectrum, people who are overly self-centred can be considered psychotic and could harm, rob or kill others for their own benefit. They are in a panic to look successful so they can love themselves. One local swindler in my community ran a Ponzi scheme. A Ponzi scheme is when you run a fictitious investment company that uses new investor money to pay high returns to old investors. This swindler would pay for the most expensive wines and food to impress others with his wealth and success, and then get people to invest with him so he could take their money. He would even rip off friends and family. He would spend this stolen money trying to impress celebrities and other people with his "greatness." Among other extravagant purchases, he paid thousands for a gold-plated seatbelt for his helicopter. After years of burning through millions of other people's dollars on luxuries, he is now in prison, separated from his wife and kids. His need to impress others (or impress himself) overrode the reality that his family and giving to others was the most important priority in his life — not taking the hard-earned money of others.

A similar scenario played out for Bernie Madoff, who ran America's largest Ponzi scheme out of New York. It may have taken over 25 years for him to be found out but now he is paying his karmic debt with horrific consequences. Mr.

Madoff is in prison and has lost a son who committed suicide, all related to his negative Ponzi scheme.

There's a big difference between giving to impress others and true giving. True giving — whether it's your money or your time — means you need nothing in return. It is a gift and this will not make the other person dependant on you. Impressing others is ego driven and usually means it's not your money or you cannot afford it and your only motive is to try to feel good about yourself, rather than help others. We usually avoid those who need to impress, unless we're taking advantage of the situation in case some money comes our way.

The only way to achieve long-term success in life is to learn to love yourself today by making healthy choices and being a giver and not a taker. Develop healthy relationships so others can depend on you and you can depend on them. If you own a business you don't want to profit off a person only once; you want them as your customer for the next 30 years. Increase your sales by creating long-term relationships with your customers. Relationships last if both partners are givers but usually break up if one is a taker.

On a larger scale, a community or neighbourhood of givers is vibrant, safe and flourishing. This community is not only full of hard workers and givers (therefore safe from vandalism, stealing, bribery or corruption) but also safe to invest in for long-term growth. A community of takers, on the other hand, is depressing and dangerous. Everyone is out for himself or herself and there will be no long-term growth.

You may feel that the law of giving doesn't always work. Those who give don't always get back, after all, or perhaps there are successful negative and self-serving individuals who override the laws of the universe and do quite well. But if you investigate the situation you will find this law is always precise. Energy comes in many forms, not just money and possessions, but in the joy of healthy relationships with friends and family. I have yet to hear of a criminal who did not get his or her just rewards, usually with horrible consequences. That drug dealer with the fancy car may only have friends with equally low karma and may be about to get beaten up, stabbed, killed or put in jail. The lawyer who is embezzling from an elderly client is about to lose his licence, be humiliated in front of all his friends and peers and get divorced from his wife with her taking all his Shih-Tzu — the family dog.

You shouldn't be surprised at how vicious the universe can be to those who harm others, but then why not? You can't expect to steal and fight and not experience consequences. I used to box for a couple of years to get in shape and I know if I punch someone I have to expect a punch back. There are many examples. Most criminals eventually get put in jail or are injured and killed. If not, they will at the very least miss out on healthy relationships, good job opportunities, and be more likely to abuse drugs and alcohol.

# STEP 2:
## DEVELOP CONFIDENCE BY AVOIDING FALSE SELF-ESTEEM

Self-esteem: a feeling of pride in
yourself, of feeling worthy.

Confidence: trusting yourself and others. The
feeling that you can walk into a new situation
and handle it, whether it's making new friends,
going to a new school or finding a job.

It's important to have a strong sense of self-esteem because
then you don't have to put others down to build yourself up.
You will get the job and the relationships you want. With
genuine self-esteem, you'll be comfortable in your own skin
and won't brag and overspend just to impress others.

Young people or anyone with low self-esteem may be using
false ways or false self-esteem to build themselves up, which
only work in the short term and can even be dangerous. Many

try to raise their confidence artificially by using drugs and alcohol, putting others down, belonging to a dominant group, having many sexual partners or by obsessing over appearance and money. These methods may seem to work at first but are only short term and have limited success. They may work as motivators to improve yourself or be social but the only long-term way to have healthy self-esteem is by being kind and giving. It is the only way to build lasting confidence because it is one of the few genuine ways to really like yourself and encourage others to like you. When you're kind, others want to be around you and so you're more inclined to like yourself and make healthy choices for your body and mind. If you become genuine it is much easier to be yourself because you have nothing to hide.

Drinking may boost your confidence but it has many side effects and is totally temporary. It's an easy way to become confident but extremely overrated. It's expensive, bad for your health and causes you to make poor judgements with sexual partners. It's extremely dangerous if you drink and drive, fight or fall while drunk.

Young people are attracted to alcohol because they see the immediate benefit of confidence. It's like a magic solution to rid you of your shyness and make you feel likeable. At a young age you might not notice the effects but eventually you will realize alcohol is not a solution and, if abused, is damaging to everyone. Just think about how much damage alcohol does to society. It causes car crashes, injuries, deaths, fighting, property damage, FAS and so on.

> *Young people have the highest rates of traffic death and injury per capita among all age groups...More 19-year-olds die or are seriously injured than any other age group... Although young people are the least likely to drive*

*impaired, the ones who do are at very high*
*risk of collision.*[1]

If you believe you have a magic confidence-maker, you will not have the incentive to find growth in your life and make the changes to find real confidence. You will be stuck with expensive and damaging drugs and alcohol.

Some people think putting others down may make them feel better about themselves and provide a jolt of confidence. In the end they don't feel any better about themselves and others may start to avoid them and their negative behaviour. "Haters" and online trolls on the Internet who spend much of their time putting down others anonymously may feel superior but not for long. Obviously this will prevent them from seeing the positive aspects of others and developing healthy relationships on or outside of the Internet.

The bully may look confident and popular to the person being bullied and to a few onlookers, but it's false. It is temporary. Eventually people and opportunity avoid you. I was bullied a fair bit, particularly in the seventh grade and, as stressful as that was, today I am most disappointed with myself because I bullied others. I still have deep regrets about the few times that I bullied other children in school. I did it for no particular reason other than to try and raise my inner confidence in front of others.

Many bullies feel lost after high school and look for other closed environments like gangs or the "underworld" where force rather than giving and kindness can be still used for influence. They then have trouble mixing with healthy individuals and avoid the real issues relating to lack of love of self.

---

1    MADD Canada. www.madd.ca/madd2/en/services/youth_services_statistics.html

Hiding behind the cloak of many by joining a group or gang is a common way to gain false self-esteem. Belonging to a group can be healthy if the organization is based on kindness and giving. If you are using the organization to feel special and part of a privileged group, however, then it will be false. You will feel confident only when you are in the group and possibly only while dominating another group. Belonging to a private club or organization that seems to have privilege might feel intoxicating, but it is only while you are comparing yourself to others and putting others down outside of the group that you feel better about yourself.

Even those who belong to a religious group may have joined it to feel important or special. This will usually be false self-esteem because it is temporary while they are in the group. They may believe they are the only ones with the one true word and get special privileges with God. They retain this confidence only when among others who have the same conviction. They may need to convince others of their beliefs in order for this to be true. The healthier religious groups are ones that gain confidence through seeing how we are all connected, serving others and treating everyone as equals. Extremist groups, who get most of their identity in their religion, country, culture, group or gang may even want to kill outsiders to maintain their feeling of superiority and false self-esteem.

Love of country may involve false self-esteem if you want your country to dominate other countries so you can feel better about yourself. It is natural to love your country and want to give back to the community that has given you so much. It is very different from getting false self-esteem because your country dominates in war, business, politics or sports. These things have nothing to do with who you are. The Nazi Party of 1930s Germany is the most obvious example of feeling dominant and powerful by belonging to a group, eventually needing to destroy or dominate others to continue getting this false self-esteem.

Members of a group feel they're special by having the same skin colour, the same team jacket, sports team, city or even the same family name if you have most of your values embedded in these things. Neo-Nazis and other radical youth groups have discovered this, but the feelings of superiority are temporary, existing only while you are in the group and busy putting down other groups. When you step out of the group, then comes the real test of whether you can feel worthy and loved when you are by yourself.

Even watching sports may include elements of unhealthy self-esteem building if you're not watching for the love of the game and the thrill of competition. Just because a sports team from your city or country beat another sports team by putting the ball or puck in the net more often, it has nothing to do with your personal greatness as a person. There should be no violence or animosity towards the other team. It's just a game. You may have temporary confidence if your team wins, but that is not really who you are. The things that matter are how you treat your co-workers, neighbours, spouse and kids.

If an alien came to visit you and bragged how great his city's sports team was at their favourite sport, and how he is related to a famous person on his planet, and how he drives one of the flashiest flying machines on his planet, or how he belongs to a special group, you wouldn't be impressed. If you are going to befriend him and be impressed by this alien "person" and want his success on our planet, you judge how he treats you and others. This dictates whether you want to hang around this being and cheer him on. If he is continually bragging, lying, putting others down and is primarily a "taker" rather than a giver, then he can go back to his home planet.

Remember!

- If you get too much of your identity and worth from the *race* you were born into then you may feel a need to put down other races to feel worthy.

- If you get too much of your identity and worth from the *culture* you were born into then you may feel a need to put down other cultures.

- If you get too much of your identity and worth from the *country* you were born into or live in then you may feel a need to dominate and put down other countries.

- If you get too much of your identity and worth from being a *man* or "manly," then you may have to put down women or try to dominate them.

- If you get too much of your identity and worth from *money* then you may put down those without money.

- If you get too much of your identity and worth from your *looks* then you may put down others who don't value looks.

- If you get too much of your identity and worth from being part of a *majority*, such as being heterosexual and traditional-family focused, then you may have to put down homosexuals and non-traditional families.

This list can go on and on but notice that these characteristics, which we constantly use to belittle each other, are mainly characteristics that we are born with and have little or no choice over. You have no choice about race, gender or sexual preference and even control over appearance is limited. We think we have total freedom of thought but ideology is passed down. We cannot help but have beliefs similar to our parents and community. How cruel and ridiculous it is to put someone down for being born with a birth defect, for being short or tall, or for being a colour they have no choice over — but some people do it all the time.

## False Self-esteem as Motivator

Particularly at a younger age, false motivators are the reason you may be jumping out of bed in the morning. You are ready to impress others and it's this human element that gives us the drive to enjoy fashion, make money and pursue social activities. This is all great, but wanting to impress others can turn into an obsession if it's just to obtain self-acceptance. You can never reach it this way. You feel you can never spend enough time in the gym to feel complete. The obsession overcomes other healthy activities such as relationships, school and work. You feel you can never be attractive enough and you may get so concerned about your appearance that you develop an eating disorder, or be so desperate for plastic surgery that you have no concern for the unhealthy trade-offs.

You may participate in sports mainly to feel better about yourself as you beat others at your chosen sport, but if you don't love the game and just use the sport for raising self-esteem, remember this only works while you are playing and winning. It is not long term.

If you want to spend hours practising to be a great rock band only to impress women to sleep with you and not for the love of music, this may motivate you for a while. If you don't have fulfilling relationships and you don't have the love and joy of giving music to others, what do you do? You may turn to drugs and alcohol to try to feel the love of self.

Needing to impress others might encourage you to take chances but if they cause injury or death it would not be a great idea. Doing dangerous stunts on your bike, street racing or chugging that extra beer won't gain you real friends. Climbing Mount Everest could be a rewarding goal but it is dangerous and may not be worth the financial cost and the risk of frostbite and death just to feel special. Examine the reasons you want to do something and be realistic about why you want to do it.

At the end of the day, the only proven way to love yourself and have others want to cheer you on and help you succeed is by being positive and giving to others. When you are kind and giving and wish the best in others, the need for false self-esteem drifts away. The need for drugs and alcohol, the need to impress others, to overspend on material goods and to obsess over your appearance will disappear. When your love of self is real, it feels absurd to want to put others down. If you are confident and you are a giver you will not feel the need to be part of a destructive group that wants to dominate others just to increase your confidence.

# STEP 3:
## REALIZE ENERGY OUT
## = ENERGY IN

*Nothing will work unless you do.*
—Maya Angelou

## The Result You Get From Past Action — Karma

If you're wondering why you aren't getting more out of life, you may not realize it's up to you to create a better life for yourself. A rock that sits and does nothing gets nothing in return. Having good things happen to you sounds like work but that is exactly what karma is. It is the return of energy or results equal to what you have put out to the community. You make things happen. Take inventory of what you've done to improve your life. What risks have you taken to meet new and positive people? What books have you read to educate yourself? What online searches have you done to learn about issues of importance to teens and even humankind.

What positive energy and value have you contributed to the community?

I was a typical young person, right out of high school, who wanted to bend the rules of the universe and have everything come easily to me. I wanted success in relationships, finances and sports without putting in the work. I thought work was for losers and I wanted the fast track. Of course I didn't have any success until I realized the universe is very fair and after years of schooling and hard work I finally understood the cliché: you get out of life what you put into it.

The energy or good karma you give to the community comes right back to you. It is happening now for many people. People in your neighbourhood or kids in your school who consciously or unconsciously understand the rules of karmic energy already have a joyous, peaceful life. They may not have everything they want, but they recognize that the success of others has been earned and they know how to achieve their own. They don't sit back and expect life to come to them. They put in the time and energy right now to be successful with friends and family, at school, with music or sports and at their jobs. Learning to be responsible for your actions and putting the time and energy into a project will dictate the success of the outcome.

The energy model is relatively simple. Giving out positive energy brings great people and opportunities to you whereas taking and negative energy drives positive people and opportunities away. This works for relationships, jobs, businesses and money. Raymond's Ice Cream Stand, with 32 flavours and soft yogurt, may last for years but Raymond's House of Typewriters that no longer creates any energy or Raymond's House of Hard Drugs that causes negative energy and harms others will inevitably have to close down.

## Dating Karma

Energy into relationships = energy out of relationships

Being attracted to someone has elements of karma. We are attracted to people who have positive energy. Someone who has worked hard at something and is now accomplished is very attractive: the musician who spent thousands of hours practising and performing, the athlete who spent hundreds of hours training and competing, the businessperson who invested many hours in the business and in building a strong company. They work hard at their craft and their work shows that they are dedicated. If these people have positive energy, we are attracted to them.

Even in high school dating there are elements of being attracted to others who put similar energy into sports or interests. If you are the type to stay at home and play video games, you will probably attract others of similar energy or no one at all if you are too isolated. If you are outgoing, involved in school activities and you volunteer for school projects, you'll be seen as more attractive because of your increased giving energy.

In a good relationship, both people would have similar karma. You get along because you have a similar education and willingness to work to get what you want. Someone who does not work very hard would not last very long with someone who is a go-getter and a hard worker. There could be resentment from both parties. And of course hard work and energy are needed for people to stay together. It takes work to learn to be accepting of another's point of view, strengths and weaknesses.

## Case Study (Tourism Karma)

On a small vacation island, the taxi drivers would rob the tourists while taking them sightseeing. The robbers got short-term results but had no long-term plan. Because of the treatment they got, tourists stopped visiting the island. The taxi drivers, the police who accepted bribes from the taxi drivers who robbed the tourists, and the locals who put up with this behaviour from their brothers, uncles, cousins or neighbours, now have very few tourists visiting. This is their self-inflicted karma. If the taxi drivers and police had been gracious and giving instead, word of mouth would have transformed the island into a safe tourist destination and there would be much more wealth for all.

The energy model, law or karma acts upon us equally, regardless of age or background. A three-year-old runs up to another three-year-old, hits him and then slips and falls while running away. That's instant negative karma. Awesome. If you plant five apple trees, you will reap the fruit of five apple trees. If you plant 10 apple trees, you will reap the fruit of 10 apple trees.

On the surface this seems too simple. We think others have avoided this law or we may hope this principle applies to everyone but ourselves. We see it as too much work to get what we want. Some of us think hard work is only for suckers and that there is a way around it.

We constantly look for ways to get around the energy law. We hope to win a lottery, get an inheritance, find a hidden treasure, write a hit song, paint a masterpiece or invent something and immediately get rich, bypassing the hard work of life. But it is impossible. No one is going to spend thousands of hours and dollars building you a house or car or anything for free. If you want things given to you without giving back, you are a taker. If you pray and want things handed to you, you are asking God to take from someone else to give to you, which isn't going to happen. The very, very few who appear to have bypassed hard work don't really exist. They probably worked harder and took more risks than you realize. The real number of young people who have won a lottery, written a hit song or inherited wealth is so incredibly small it's not worth mentioning. Even if they do receive riches, they still have to work hard to hold on to it and must continue to give to their community or risk losing their money and/or being pulled into drugs and alcohol in their idle time, making their lives worse.

As a kid I remember seeing a movie called *The Doberman Gang* about some guys who trained their dogs to rob a bank. It was a cheesy 1970s kids' movie but you couldn't help but cheer for the guys and hope they stole the money so they would never have to go to school or work again. I was ready to start training dogs. Many movies glorify the shortcut but it is an illusion — there isn't one in real life. Every successful person worked hard for what they have and if we find out someone has taken without giving, we want to punish them, usually putting them in jail, or avoiding them.

The energy model is evident everywhere. Someone who spends 2,000 hours practising the piano will, with the same instruction, be much better at playing than someone who only practised for 200 hours. The athlete who trains harder and longer at a sport will be better at it than another athlete who trains less. There are variables that add or subtract from the experience, such as the efficiency of the practising and skills of the coaches or instructors, but the results still adhere to the principle of energy out = energy in. Wayne Gretzky — known as The Great One — is considered by many to be the best hockey player of all time. He put in the hours, practised at a young age (his dad put a rink in the backyard) and constantly played at a high level thanks to coaching from his father and other coaches and from playing against much older kids. No one has shot more practise balls in golf before the age of 18 than Tiger Woods, a record 11 time PGA Player of the Year. The best player on any team is almost always the first to show up for practice and the last one to leave. There are some exceptions to this rule because of body size but you cannot deny the effort-to-success correlation.

The more hours spent learning, teaching, parenting, painting, sailing, hunting or farming, will pay off with more skill in those areas. The more hours you work, the more you get paid or will get paid with an eventual promotion in your profession. The calories (energy) you eat minus the calories you burn will dictate your weight. The time you spend on your social life will dictate your satisfaction.

There is a whole industry of books and seminars claiming to offer shortcuts but there are none that compare with putting in the hours. To be an architect with 20 years of experience means becoming an architect and working 20 years. It could be years — thousands of hours — before you are a successful doctor, engineer, businessperson, musician, actor, parent or athlete. How could it be any other way? Everyone started with nothing. For everyone the path started with one step. Some of the biggest restaurateurs in my town started years ago with just a vending cart. The trick is to be comfortable starting small and learning to grow. Eventually it will come to be.

How fair would it be if the longer you worked at something the worse you got? Could you imagine if the more hours you practised with your band, the worse you sounded? It's just not possible. It may be frustrating to know that it takes over 20 years to have the sound and the success of the top rock bands but do you think they regret their journey? They probably have a real fondness for their early days. And their ability to respect each other's differences has rewarded them with longevity as a band.

This principle works in households, companies and countries. The more educated and hardworking the individual, the more the family, the company and the country will have. The energy model also works in reverse. Negative energy caused by war, conflict, corruption, lying and stealing will reduce the health of the family, company or country. Therefore, those who take from society in the form of stealing, corruption, lying and living in low karma usually miss out on healthy relationships, a healthy body and healthy finances.

I have never met anyone who did not deserve his or her joy. Most people have worked hard educating themselves, improving their relationship with their spouse and raising their children. Most are very generous with their time at the workplace and outside the workplace, with friends and with the community. Many people right this minute are enjoying extreme happiness in their lives and they are not necessarily wealthy or extraordinary. They just give out goodness and get it straight back.

Of all the ways to increase one's karma, smiling is the most effective and the easiest. People who smile are just beaming positive energy. Doors open for them because people like to be around them. Smiling immediately makes others smile, becoming a chain reaction of good energy. When you walk into a room, feel glad to be alive, and smile. A smile tells people you acknowledge them. You are glad to see them and be in their company. It tells others that you have an open heart and you don't judge. It tells others you are accepting, gentle, friendly, approachable and considerate. You would be surprised how much happier people who smile are, and how much more likely to be invited out for social activities and given job promotions. If you don't smile, your heart is not open. You appear to be judgmental, self-centred and insecure, with no concern for others or looking for advantage by being intimidating. Those who believe in God see God in others and impress those around you.

There is a lady who used to power walk through my neighbourhood every day. She marches by with such a grim face and never smiles at the neighbours working in their yard. It is very hard for me to bounce positive energy back to her because she is not open to it. What would happen to her mindset if she walked with a huge smile on her face and if she acknowledged and smiled at every person she passed? She would get a smile right back. Just think how much happier and energized she would be after her walk. Multiply this by every person every day and you can see the power of a smile. How many years have I wasted not smiling as much as I should have and not giving out positive energy so others could bounce positive energy right back to me?

## Why do Bad Things Sometimes Happen to People Giving out Good Energy?

I could throw a tennis ball into a crowd and bean one person on the head. That person did not have bad karma — it was just a random throw. Bad things can randomly happen to everyone regardless of how we live but this is the chance we take, living on this planet. The planet is a complex organism that experiences lightning, wild animals, fires, tornadoes, hurricanes and earthquakes. Humans have heavily populated the Earth, introduced large machinery and new technology, and farmed and changed the land, and there will be natural stress points in nature. All we can do is reduce the odds of bad things happening to ourselves, graciously accept when things happen that are out of our control, and understand that bad things are part of living on a heavily populated and vibrant planet.

The earthquakes in Japan, Haiti, New Zealand, Pakistan and other areas are not because of bad karma. They were simply caused by a shifting of the Earth's crust, which is happening all the time. All we can try to do is reduce the effect of earthquakes by not living near those areas or by building safer buildings.

> *I've failed over and over and over again in my life*
> *and that is why I succeed.*
> —Michael Jordan

Sometimes it seems as though something bad is happening to you such as the loss of a job or the break-up of a relationship. This is a perfect time to learn from the situation and use the experience to progress to bigger opportunities such as a better job or a healthier relationship. If you have good karma, seemingly negative events are most likely going to lead to a better situation. They may seem like setbacks but are only minor changes that help you focus on what's important in life. If your karma is fairly low and you know it, then you must not be surprised to learn that you have put yourself in a particularly poor situation. If you're selling drugs, you should not be surprised when you're surrounded by people with low karma and you risk theft, injury or even death. If you have not educated yourself, then you should not be surprised that your job prospects are reduced and your pay is low.

Even car accidents are inevitable but can be reduced. It's quite amazing that most of us drive around in gigantic metal vehicles that weigh 3000 pounds and can accelerate to 100 mph in seconds, yet there are relatively few accidents. But we take a risk for the luxury of getting around in such large machines. If you get hit by a drunk driver or by someone running a red light, it is not your karma that attracted the accident. It's just the risk we take every day, living in large cities and jostling with the thousands of cars in traffic. All we can do is continue to promote safe driving and reduce the odds of having an accident.

But it is your bad energy that causes you to have an accident when you drink and drive, speed, don't follow the rules of the road, race other cars, drive in an overloaded vehicle or drive a vehicle that is faulty or poorly maintained. Then you are at major risk of an accident and injury because of the size and speed of the vehicles. All we can do is slow down, be defensive drivers, avoid drinking or texting while driving and expect other people to make occasional mistakes, covering for them as you hope they will cover for you if you make a poor judgement call on the road.

## You Can Reduce the Chance of Bad Things Happening to You Today

- You never get addicted to a drug if you never try it.

- You never get sick from drugs or alcohol if you don't abuse them.

- You never get addicted to smoking if you never smoke.

- You never get a speeding ticket if you never speed.

- You never get in a car accident caused by alcohol-induced poor decisions if you don't drink and drive.

- You cannot get pregnant if you abstain from sex or use birth control properly.

# Why Does Lying Cause Such Negative Karma?

Lying always causes problems because people may never trust you again and because it is misinformation. It is done to sway a decision in a preconceived direction. You feel you know the proper outcome, so you change the facts. But the proper outcome only comes about when factual information is made available. Influential people in government, religion and business as well as teachers and parents need to avoid lying at all costs. The end doesn't justify the means.

The broken trust and the misinformation can cause more damage than the truth would have, and it comes back to haunt you. I try not to lie to anyone in my family. I may withhold some information from my kids that they don't need to know but I never tell them a big lie or made-up story about why they should brush their teeth or eat properly. I only give accurate information to the best of my ability to maintain trust so they can make informed decisions. Leaders in all walks of life who lie whether at work, at your church or in government, do you no favours by lying and it always comes back to harm them. Lying causes bad energy and results in bad karma. Even if you think you're doing something right, you're robbing another person of accurate information. Countries that waste energy lying and distorting information for the "greater good" end up harming the community instead. A lie has to be covered up with another lie, which has to be covered up with another lie. Honest disclosure brings about positive results. The more honest the information, the more positive is the energy to the community. This is where understanding and healthy relationships are formed.

## There Has Never Been and Never Will be a Successful Criminal

Just think of the negative lives of today's drug gangs. They usually live in filth, risk getting killed and injured, and have an unhealthy body and relationships. It's usually a group of men who want to take instead of give, with disastrous results. They don't offer anything to the community; they just want to take. Are they building roads, houses, schools and hospitals? Are they raising healthy families? Are they helping with mining, forestry, farming and the oil and gas industries? No. They just want people addicted to drugs so they can profit from the distribution of drugs. With no concern for others, they get hooked into using drugs and alcohol to cover up their negative energy. Any remaining money will be spent on overpriced possessions such as flashy clothes and cars to promote a false image that has no inner substance. This carries over into their social life and results in unhealthy relationships with family and friends. If they stay alive, they will have a stressful and continual relationship with the criminal justice system as they go in and out of jail or prison. They will develop a long criminal record and spend much of their money on lawyers, fines, drugs and alcohol for their own use.

## Karma and the Environment

The good news about being kind to the environment is that you almost always get rewarded for doing so. If you buy something without packaging, it's usually cheaper than buying something heavily packaged. You get rewarded for buying quality over cheap products. Many of the low-quality dollar store products my wife and I have bought for the kids break even before we get them home and they go straight into landfill. Reducing the need for landfills and setting areas aside for nature provides a healthier, happier place to live.

If you ride your bike instead of driving a car, you are saving thousands of dollars a year. Reducing the amount of driving you do and the size of your vehicle saves you incredible amounts of money. I think some commuters would be shocked to know how much of their disposable income is used in getting to work and back. If you are paying for parking as well, you really need to crunch the numbers and think about taking public transportation or changing jobs so you can live closer to your work. If you can stop throwing money at the oil companies, they will stop searching and extracting oil from the earth.

Public transportation is the cornerstone of a healthy community because it is great for the environment and it allows everyone, regardless of their financial means, to have access to all areas of the city for work or for personal reasons. Wealth increases in the community because fewer cars mean fewer people working to pay for their cars or road infrastructure. There is so much less energy being used when a subway or train system delivers one million people to work than one million cars. More time and energy can go into other ventures and be spent with family and friends. The city is that much more liveable.

One of the main ways to help the environment is by stabilizing population growth. No one wants to tackle the difficult cultural implications with our current family models but with exponential population growth, this is probably our greatest concern as we continue to overpopulate, pollute and destroy our living environment. Think of our Earth as an island with limited room and resources, which it is. It is finite and if we take from the Earth faster than the Earth can renew itself, then we only harm ourselves. There will be real consequences. Those who deny this selfishly don't want to change their lifestyle, with little concern for others today or in the future.

We are much too apathetic, allowing thousands of children to live in slums or work in factories. We are much too comfortable, allowing animals to go extinct. We have very little incentive to stop burning fossil fuels millions of times more quickly than it took to make them. We are too nonchalant about increased cancer rates and other health problems that come from not looking after our land but this is all self-induced. It's never too late to make a difference and support issues you find a passion for.

## What if I Have Already Done Something Damaging to Another? Can I Change my Karma?

If you have harmed another person in a serious way, then you have to deal with it. If you ask for forgiveness from those you harmed, you help heal them and yourself. I think the old TV show *My Name is Earl* is on to something. The main character goes through a checklist of things he has done wrong to others and tries to make amends, with good results. The sooner the other person can heal, the sooner you can heal and allow yourself to move on. It's not something that can be left to fester. Forgiveness is possible. There have been amazing instances of a mother forgiving her child's killer after a time, when she knows deep in her heart that the killer is sorry and has changed his ways. Things will never be the same but it is the least negative aspect of an extremely tragic situation.

It is not too late to stop any bad behaviour. Even if it takes months or even years to repay the karmic debt, why make it last longer? Stop lying, stealing, embezzling or abusing drugs and alcohol. Stop it today. Even if you've been doing it for years, the sooner you stop it the sooner you will be leading a happier life. You may be back into positive karma territory faster than you think.

# STEP 4:

## STOP THE BLAME; YOU MAKE THINGS HAPPEN

Blaming others takes the ability to change away from you so that no learning takes place. It allows you to make excuses instead of growing and making a change. You miss the connection between your behaviour and its outcome. You may replace feelings of frustration and powerlessness with food, drugs and alcohol, gambling or other vices.

It's almost as simple as there being two types of people in the world. One person blames others, doesn't take responsibility, doesn't make the appropriate changes and is negative to be around. This person has limited success and is not grateful for his amazing chance at life. Then there is another person who never blames anyone else for her predicament, is grateful for what she has, and takes the appropriate action to change a situation for greater success. This person is positive, grateful, successful and great to be around. This person understands the elements of karma or energy and is willing to work for what she wants, while others complain about what they don't have.

Become accountable for your life. It is futile to blame your parents, the government, other religions, other races, your neighbours or your boss. It leaves you thinking that you have no say in your life and that's just not true. When you walk out the front door of your house, it's 100% you who makes the decisions.

There are people and even entire nations still blaming injustices from past generations for their misfortunes. When do you stop blaming? Only when you realize there is no one to blame will you learn to make the change yourself. You live in the present and your world is your responsibility.

People from countries that feel they are given no power by their leadership, whether or not this is actually the case, will sometimes resort to violence or join radical opposition groups that promote violence; however, long-lasting change can only be achieved peacefully. It may take years but even with a dictator, healthy change takes place without violence. The Berlin Wall did eventually come down, but peacefully. It takes extreme patience. Ghandi, Nelson Mandela, Martin Luther King Jr. and others have proven peaceful protest and education is the only way to create long-lasting peace. Syria and every single other civil war has proven that violence brings violence.

It's the front lines that make the difference. You do what you can do in your own backyard. If you work for the government, you can promote a culture of transparency, free of corruption. If you work for someone else, be an honest and hard-working employee, and get the good karma of working for a successful business with job stability and advancement. If you own a business, promote good karma by providing a healthy working environment for your employees and support for the community. If you're raising a family, ensure that your kids are healthy and well educated. Policy change for a community starts with you. Little bits of your energy slowly creep into the energy of those with more decision-making power. Do what you can do in your own workplace and at home. When others see your success, the community will follow.

# STEP 5:

## BE AWARE OF THE COMPARE

If you feel better when others fail, you are comparing. If you are going to use the strategy of comparing yourself with others so you can look down on those who seem to have less than you in order to feel better about yourself, then this comparison strategy will work against you. You will eventually feel sad, as there is always someone who has more than you. There has never been a time in history when we have had such a wealth of knowledge, technology, health care and entertainment that was available only to the richest people a few decades ago. Nevertheless, sadness still exists because we compare ourselves to others who seem to have more things and better relationships.

We forget that on TV and in movies, most 18-year-olds are being played by successful 25-year-olds and professional 25- to 55-year-old writers are writing their dialogue. We constantly feel that we don't measure up to others. It seems there is always someone smarter, more talented and more attractive.

Comparing and trying to keep up with our neighbours can be a great benchmark and motivator of self-improvement but not if we use comparisons to feel worthy of loving ourselves. Internal love and acceptance is the way. There are people who have won major championships or Academy Awards, earned millions of dollars, are extremely good-looking and have the "perfect" mate but are still unhappy.

If we get deep into the game of comparing ourselves to others then we will have to put others down to feel better about ourselves. Not everyone can be the best at anything or everything, so to avoid feeling inferior, some have to bring others down to their level by pointing out all their shortcomings. If you've done this, it may help you to feel good about yourself temporarily but you cannot trick yourself. Deep down you will not feel confident and not worthy of success.

Be aware and try not to compare yourself to others, as it can be very damaging to your thoughts. Instead, be really grateful for what you have. If you analyse your day and think of all the little experiences you witnessed, you will be thankful to exist on this amazing planet. Just being alive is a mind blower. Take the time to look at the complexities of an insect or the flight of a bird. Feel your breath come out of your amazing body. Look around at all the complexities of how machines and technology work. Smile at someone and get a smile back. It's very hard to be mean to others and put them down when you realize all that you have.

## The Problem of Comparing Your Present Life to a Future Fantasy Life

We tend to be hard on ourselves and get angry when we compare ourselves to an imagined future life that is a fantasy about where we should be. It will almost always disappoint. How can our imagination ever match reality? There are just too many variables for the brain to foresee the outcome. One is based on assumptions and the other is based on reality. We can fantasize about being a famous actor, singer, musician, sports star, politician or astronaut, or about saving the world. This is good because it helps us push ourselves to greatness even if the outcome is different from what we had originally thought. The trouble is that we can expect too much and disappoint ourselves; this can lead to anger and depression.

We get into fantasy issues when we imagine our boyfriend or girlfriend and how they should behave. We fantasize about how much money we should have or what job we should have. We have all witnessed terrible singers on TV singing competitions that must have fantasized their singing contract before competing and cannot believe they are not talented. You have to enjoy life right now and enjoy the process, not just the outcome, because the odds of winning or being number one in many areas of life are miniscule. There is one gold medal for each Olympic event, one state champion and one actor chosen for each role in a movie, but should the thousands who tried out be disappointed? Absolutely not. Participation in these activities in life comes with a huge learning experience that has nothing to do with winning or even the sport or competition. It's also about developing friendships, enjoying the activity and knowing that success comes from "energy out."

Comparing yourself to others has its place — to have guidance about how life could be — but it should not be an obsession. Each person is so different, maturing at different levels, each with skill sets to provide many ways to contribute to the community. This diversification creates a vibrant community and everyone benefits from the differences. If you really must compare yourself to others, you have to realize the fact that hard work gets results and with everything there are trade-offs. Many successful business people sacrifice family time. With more fame comes less privacy. With money comes more responsibilities. This is why when you are grateful for where you are in life, you will find you are right on schedule. Life is not a race and is not really that short. We may easily live for 80 or more years and all you really need to be concerned about is nurturing your health.

## Be Grateful

Why do we want everything today? Is it so we can finally love ourselves and feel worthy of existence? Then love yourself today. Be thankful about the process of a planet forming for billions of years for us all to enjoy today.

Gratitude is almost the opposite of comparing. It's very important because it's hard to be sad or depressed if you realize all you have instead of comparing yourself to others and realizing what you don't have. Usually it's more like the glass is only 98% full and we get depressed that the glass is two per cent empty. If you just think of your ability to exist, to breathe, to see, smell, touch, taste and hear, that should be enough for you. Could a person 100 years ago be happy if s/he had none of the material goods we have today? Should I be unhappy with myself if I don't have the inventions of the future?

At the end of every day, write in a gratitude journal. Write down even the smallest things to be thankful for and I guarantee you will go to bed with a smile on your face.

*Be thankful for what you have; you'll end up having more.*
*If you concentrate on what you don't have, you will never,*
*ever have enough."*
—Oprah Winfrey

# STEP 6:
## THINK LONG TERM

If you force someone to give you half of his chocolate bar, then in the short term you may be successful. Initially you will get a result — free chocolate. But because the person who gave you the chocolate bar will stay away from you or not carry one around anymore, you will never get another chocolate bar from that person even if you get the chance to use force or threaten him. Alternatively, if you are kind to someone and offer something in return, then it's a win-win situation and that person will gladly share today and any day.

Some of the poorest people in the world are in that position because they operate in survival mode. They only plan on what it takes to eat in the next hour or day. Sadly, they experience such extreme poverty that they aren't in a position to see the big picture and realize that a decision they make today affects them months from now. How fortunate that many in the world have parents or a social infrastructure that can look after the young for years until they are ready to look after themselves and in the meanwhile get highly educated.

Not thinking long term can be dangerous. Short-term thinking means we eat unhealthily, smoke and use drugs without thinking of the long-term health effects. Thinking short term means we have affairs without considering our spouse or children. It has us taking $10 from the cash register without seeing the ripple effect of damage we are causing to our employers and our feelings of self-worth. Rape is a few minutes of selfish pleasure and a lifetime of regret. Drinking and driving or fighting are short-term decisions with possible long-term consequences. If you were really thinking of how your actions could have long-term implications, you probably wouldn't have gotten pregnant, said something mean to a friend or tried that addictive drug or stolen something.

Those who think long-term are more likely to make healthier decisions in all areas of their lives. They look after their health, drink in moderation and stay away from drugs, educate themselves and have better financial planning, all while enjoying the present. To think long term doesn't have to be boring and we shouldn't need pain to feel alive. Is it boring to sleep well at night, have a body free of injury or disease, have functional relationships with others and have financial freedom?

If we don't think long term we are being very selfish to our future self. You can be drinking and having a good time and say, "I'm going to have a good time now. I don't care about my future self. I'll worry about my hangover tomorrow." When tomorrow comes and you are puking, you wish your past self wasn't so selfish. It's the same for not exercising enough or over-eating. What you eat and how much you exercise directly affects your future body.

Thinking long term does not mean you don't enjoy the present. It just means you are aware that you may live for over 80 years and your future self is depending on you. Your future self is hoping you are looking after your body, getting your brain educated and not damaging it with drugs so you can charge top dollar for your skills and make healthy choices about relationships. It is hoping you will look after your body so you won't have to rely on prescription drugs (that are only minimal help and have many side effects) to counteract the damage to your body and brain in the future. It means hoping you are saving money and investing it so you won't have to work so hard when your body can't work as much.

## Wait to Have Kids

When it comes to thinking long term there is nothing more important than the decision to raise a child because it is at least an 18-year commitment. Think about it – 18 years! Sex has the biggest consequence possible. You do not want a baby when you are young. Looking after a baby is much harder than you could ever imagine. Babies deserve to be raised by mature parents that are committed.

Being responsible for raising a child will be the most rewarding experience of your life, because of the sacrifice and hard work required to raise this helpless being. If you are not totally committed, it can be a negative experience. The child is not the negative experience. Instead it is the juggling of time, financial stress and relationship stress that comes with being a parent. You have to be psychologically and financially established to undertake this momentous experience.

Worldwide, poverty is inevitable because the parents were too young and didn't plan for it. The young parents didn't allow sufficient time to build up their skills and become educated and financially stable. Having children is extremely expensive because of the child's needs but it also means you cannot work as much outside the home and the child takes almost all your time inside the home.

Many are having kids when they shouldn't be: in times of war, in cities that are over-populated and polluted, when they are extremely poor, and when they don't have a committed partner. You don't need to be rich to be a great parent but you do have to provide basic needs and healthy choices. Some families are so poor that their kids have to hunt through garbage dumps for food. Some families are so destitute they sell their kids for money or let them marry when they are still children. Cultures and religions have to take responsibility for not encouraging birth control and the confusion over the idea that having children is the only way to make you whole.

How ridiculous it is that some parents, mostly men, do not follow through with raising their children when it is one of the truest ways to find joy — helping another human become independent. It covers almost every aspect of this book to make you a complete and happy human by learning selflessness, the joy of giving, increasing your confidence (because of your contribution to the community, which usually translates into financial wealth), and all this productive time steers you away from drug and alcohol abuse.

This is the hardest time in your life to think long term when all you can really think about is how to get short-term love and acceptance from yourself and others this weekend. But at least be aware of it. You are going to be alive for over 3,100 more weekends and think how glad your future self will be that you looked after your body, and put in the time to educate yourself to be a great parent and get that great paying job. It's not easy to think long term when you're young but if you can be kind to your body today, your future self will really appreciate it.

# STEP 7:
## KNOW YOUR EGO

*As the ego becomes strong it starts surrounding*
*intelligence like a thick layer of darkness.*
*Intelligence is light, ego is darkness.*
—Taoist Principle

What is the ego? There are many interpretations of the ego, but it is basically the part of the brain that is more concerned with itself than others, as it is obsessed with self-image and self-preservation. Ego may go against the main part of my book and many other philosophies, which is "put others first," but it has a place. It just wants to make sure you look after yourself and your tribe or family so you stay alive, which includes passing on your DNA and making more of your species, and it just wants to be noticed in a world of billions.

Unfortunately, this part of the brain tends to be pre-programmed and rigid, and if you are too concerned with yourself and those close to you, no one else will want to be around you or your tribe. Ego may make you want to look after your own kids and grandkids over others but you would be selfish to want to harm or not to be concerned about other children, as in times of armed conflict. Ego may be part of the reason you want to procreate but it may not be a good idea if you are living in extreme poverty and can't look after your children. Ego may make you aware of how you dress and your appearance to impress others, but it can be unhealthy for you to be obsessed with appearance.

The ego can be a great motivator for an individual as he tries harder at sports to impress the coach and others. You may need a bit of ego to be motivated to be the best player on the basketball team, the chemistry student with the highest mark, or the lead in the school play. But the problem with ego is when it takes things too far and has no concern for others. It only wants the accolades and the short-term love. You want healthy motivation for the love of the game or for the love of competition, not just for the admiration.

How much healthier it is to pursue the challenge to be the best because you enjoy doing your best, not just impressing others. Be proud of your hard work but realize that is not who you are. You still need to be giving and kind to others to get love of self.

If you are obsessed with impressing others, you may be behaving dangerously. Racing cars and fighting may not be the healthiest activities. It is not worth risking your precious life at these activities if you are doing it only to impress or feel special.

Young ego wants the title of "most desired girl in the tribe or even the world." When teenage girls fantasize about being the only love of the latest heartthrob, their young ego wants this title, to be chosen over millions of others, to feel special. Even as adults we have all fantasized about getting asked on stage to sing with our favourite music star or fantasized about what it would be like to be rich and famous. Feel worthy because you exist and are kind to others, not by being more special or better than others.

## The Ego after a Breakup

It's not easy to break up with someone or to be let go. To think you're going to date only one person is very unlikely. You will experience breakups, but they can be done with good karma. Do it by being honest and realistic. It doesn't matter how great you are, there are so many variables that individuals are looking for in a partner that a match is almost impossible. And even when you think you have a match, the variables change as the person grows and changes. A breakup is not a failure on anyone's part, just an important growing experience.

Why is it that when someone breaks up with you it is so painful? It's probably more because of your ego than anything, but the pain is still real. You haven't been in this situation before and you had put very high expectations and fantasies on how the relationship was going to be. You have fallen in love because you can't believe you found someone who accepts you for just being you and you assume you will never find anyone better. Now with the break up, your ego begins to doubt its ability to attract another.

At the extremes of the ego, the most psychotic person, overly concerned with self, has been known to kill the person that rejects him. The ego cannot believe it is being rejected and it must destroy the person who is promoting this lie that he is not worthy of love. Mid-level psychotic behaviour is slashing your ex-partner's tires or stealing his cat.

The healthiest response would be to realize that you are sad because of this loss. This is natural. Just be aware of ego. Loss is sad for everyone and all we can do is talk it over with friends and look forward to the real-life experiences we are going to have with new partners, rather than stew over what our fantasies or ego had predicted.

It is sad that we need women's shelters to protect women from violent men who cannot handle the breakup because of ego, and sad that many divorces end in hate and dysfunction. Thousands of dollars may be needed for lawyers to handle the divorce and usually very little consideration is given to what's best for the kids. The ego only cares for what's best for itself and for defending its image over the cost and concern for others.

## Try Not Being so Defensive About Advice

Many successful athletes are successful because they can override ego and be what is called "coachable." They buy into the coach's methods and listen and do whatever s/he says with an almost blind faith. With their trust and hard work, they or their team are very successful. A coach does not make the athlete powerless. On game day the player does the execution but the coach provides the structure and pressure so the athlete can do his best.

I couldn't stand it when my mother gave me advice. It felt as though she was not accepting of me. One thing she would continually do is to tell me to stop slouching at the dinner table and sit up straight. I couldn't stand it. I would sometimes slouch just to get her upset in spite of myself. We do this all the time and do the opposite of what others suggest even though we know they are right. It's called passive resistance and it's a no-win position.

Our parents, teachers, friends and society have been telling us what to do all our lives, and we would rather harm ourselves than be told how to live. It seems that our egos are defending our identity when really they are not related. Doing the opposite of what you are told just for the sake of it doesn't make sense. You should make the best decision for yourself.

It was very difficult for me to stop slouching because then it seemed as though my mother had won and her putting me down was justified. I had to consciously remind myself that in this instance, standing up straight was for my own good. It was healthier for the body and it looked better. To slouch, overspend or overeat because others tell you not to, doesn't make sense. Parents are probably too controlling at times and may not always know what's best. Many times they may want you to appear impressive because it makes them look good as parents. But doing the opposite isn't a solution. Do what's best for yourself. Kids who have strong relationships with their parents are probably more likely to accept advice from them and not feel they are having their power or identity compromised.

What happens if your parents are poor role models? They don't practise what they preach, nag at getting you to change, and dominate most of your choices so you feel no empowerment. What happens if you don't understand why teachers and authority figures seem so constricting? You may take up smoking and do something reckless to try to get some of that power back. Smoking, speeding, painting graffiti and vandalism all give temporary feelings of empowerment but are damaging to your life and will harm you instead.

I was fortunate to have a life coach for a few months in my early thirties. She gave me a huge push in a relatively short time. I was open and willing and in a few months she helped me get over blaming my parents for my problems and helped me with my confidence and feelings of self-worth. The result was that I applied for a new job that paid me much more than I was previously making.

Reading books, using counsellors and coaches, listening to others and doing online research are great ways to learn. We hate advice; our egos can't stand it. The ego thinks it knows it all, but it probably knows nothing more than how it was programmed for thinking how life should be from reading teen books and watching teen sitcoms and movies when you were younger. If you can learn to override that delicate ego and intellectualize the big picture, you can learn lots from others. Unless an adult is trying to take advantage of you sexually or financially, which of course is possible, most adults have no ulterior motive but are kind souls with lots of life experience to pass on.

Those who defend their ego the most probably need the most help. Try spending one day a week not defending yourself. If someone at work, at school or at home criticizes you, just listen and think about it. This does not mean you necessarily agree, it just means today you will listen to everyone. This will force you to listen instead of immediately turning off your brain and letting your precious ego defend you to the death or until the other person walks away. Occasionally, not defending yourself will show you that this behaviour is not at all painful. It does not take away your power or make you weak. You may start to see other points of view more clearly and it can actually make the day less stressful. You will not have to butt heads with anyone and others may even want to hang out with you.

## Feel Worthy not Special

Feeling worthy is very different from feeling special. You are at your best when you feel worthy and loved, and believe you are deserving of goodness. You will make great choices. You don't need to put others down, you don't need to brag, and you are giving and kind. You live in the moment and are grateful for where you are right now in life.

You can be at your worst when your ego wants to feel special. Being overly concerned with yourself and desperately trying to feel special may mean you put yourself above others. It's almost childlike behaviour. You elbow your way to the front of the line, get upset if you aren't picked first, take the biggest slice of pizza, walk into a room and think it's all about you. You don't listen to others and only care about your own opinions. Ideal parenting would be to teach feelings of worth over feelings of being special and that you deserve more than others. (Daddy I want you to get me an Oompa Loompa right away!)

If you love and accept yourself, you are gracious and loving to others and experience the positive results of kindness and non-judgement. You understand that everyone's time and opinions are valuable. You graciously wait for your turn in line. You gladly let others merge into traffic while driving. A community of giving is much more functional and happy than a community of taking.

After tragedies like hurricanes, tsunamis, floods or earthquakes, I'm always impressed by those who considerately wait in line for food handouts and reach out to help each other, instead of those who grab and loot with an attitude of everyone for him or herself.

If you strive to be special rather than worthy, you want an unfair advantage over others. You may only help others if it's clearly to your advantage. You might be tempted to join a political or religious group for an advantage over others instead of to be giving. You may be tempted to join one of those groups that use special symbols, have special handshakes, and wear special robes like the Templar Knights, the Illuminati, and the Masons, because you think they have special power and insight.

The fact that you want these powers reveals a lot about your character. Any belief system that includes wanting a holy grail, having whatever you want, taking advantage of others, or living forever is all a matter of ego.

We are all guilty of wanting advantage over others in some way (perhaps better equipment than the other team when playing sports), but it's not right to join the board of directors, the union executive or a political party not to make the company or the world a better place, but to gain financially.

You may not go to great lengths to feel special, but you want to feel special in some way. It helps you strive to be good at something no one else can do. Unfortunately, it can be unhealthy and even dangerous if you want to climb the highest mountain or set that world record juggling chain saws.

If your ego has you so obsessed with yourself, at the most extreme you are psychotic. You think it's okay to take from and hurt others, lie, steal or cheat for the benefit of you or your family. You may even kill others if it means improving your finances or increasing your artificial image of yourself. You need to get rid of those who think less of you. Perhaps you are a psychotic who wants to kill someone, to temporarily feel superior, even if it means a lifetime in jail.

I don't mean to diminish the complexities of depression but one element of it might be the over-concern with self, as you think all your issues are the only ones in the world. Add in comparing yourself to others and your expectations of where you think you should be in life and it is hard to feel good about yourself.

You may feel worthy most of the time and are not overly self-centred but even at the best of times you will rely on external values to feel good about yourself. You look to money, your partner or your image to improve how you feel about yourself. You may spend too much time obsessed with your looks or you may brag and put others down to raise yourself up.

It starts almost immediately when you are just a toddler and you learn that if you hurt your little brother or sister you feel better about yourself. You may feel more deserving of a parent's love. It continues throughout your school life in the schoolyard as you isolate and put down others and join groups and bully to feel superior. Of course this is disastrous. Those who are negative and put others down end up hating themselves and thus the negative spiral continues.

Pinch yourself. You're alive and worthy but not special. If you need to feel special you can come across as self-centred and irritating. You don't have to brag about the celebrity autograph and your giant gas-guzzling vehicle. Touching your lucky hat three times isn't influencing the football game, happening halfway across the country, as you watch it on T.V. You aren't so special that you can take advantage of that drunk girl at a party because you're a star on the sports team. You don't have to chop down that 400-year-old tree for your personal use or financial gain, and cancel the joy of others seeing it. You don't need to sneak a chunk of stone off one of the Great Pyramids while visiting it to feel special and a part of this civilization. [For many of life's answers just ask yourself, "What would happen to the world if everyone did that?"] You don't need to join that group or stranger that promises to make you feel special. You don't need to use brain-altering drugs to temporarily feel in the present and one of a kind. You don't need seven kids because you're such an amazing specimen, but you are lovable, unique and worthy and you deserve to be on this amazing planet just as much as the next person.

It's very important every once in a while to be away from city lights and look at the night sky and see the billions of stars. When you do this or look at pictures of our amazing Earth taken from space, it helps you realize the grand scheme of things. You may be just the subject of chance, but your existence is still pretty amazing.

# STEP 8:
## INCREASE FINANCIAL WEALTH

$1 million worth of work = $1 million

Skill/Education x Tools/Machine x Risk x
Hours Worked = Work Value or Wealth

The only way others are going to give you $1 million is by you giving them $1 million worth of value. People are paying for your energy. Whether it's for your time, knowledge or physical or mental value, they will not give up their work credits easily unless they get something back.

If you receive without giving, you are basically stealing. You may want money without giving anything in return but it will never happen unless you get it as a gift or inheritance, which is very rare at a young age and not always a good thing. Only $1 million worth of work gets you $1 million. If you are given money for nothing, such as an inheritance, it may take away your drive to make your own money. The only time to accept money without giving something back is if you have no choice and have to depend on others because of a temporary job layoff or you have physical or developmental disabilities.

If you take without earning you will be dependent on those who give you the free money and you will not change your behaviour. That is why those who take from the community are often the poorest. Others will only give you the minimum amount that you need to survive on. It is not easy for others to part with their hard-earned money.

Money is not necessary for happiness but if you want something, you have to exchange your skill or this currency, which represents your work. It's not surprising that Bill Gates is a billionaire because he and his software company have enabled computers to do billions of hours of work in the global community. I may not agree with the high pay of some sport, music and movie stars but we pay them through our demand to see them. The more we want to watch them play, sing or act, the more they can charge.

Notice in the following examples at different restaurants that as more energy gets put into the product, the value goes up and a higher price can be charged. The public is willing to pay more, because no one else will do that much work without getting paid for it.

> Restaurant 1 sells factory-made cookies for $1 each.

> Restaurant 2 makes homemade chocolate chip cookies for $2 each.

> Restaurant 3 makes homemade sandwiches for $4 each.

> Restaurant 4 sells hot lunches for $8 each.

> Restaurant 5 sells full dinners for $16 each.

Restaurant 6 sells very labour-intensive gourmet meals for $32 each.

## Five Main Ways to Increase Your Wealth

1. Raise your value by educating or training yourself to make your skills more desirable.

2. Increase your ability to use a machine, tool or computer program that will do work for others.

3. Take (non-dangerous and legal) risks that others aren't willing to take, entitling you to charge more for your services when opening up your own business or changing the light bulb at the top of the power pole (with safety harness).

4. Work longer hours.

5. Be comfortable starting small and foregoing instant pleasure for long-term gain.

There are no shortcuts to wealth. If a particular building takes 15,000 hours of work to build, including all the parts that are processed and built ahead of time (lumber and windows, metal pipes and wires), then it takes 15,000 hours of work to build. Until technology can get the job done faster, that's it. It is a firm reality. Many have made millions through their knowledge of technology or their skill set but you don't always see the time and effort it took to get there. An "overnight" success usually takes thousands of hours of work and lots of risk to make the product or skills so valuable that the person can charge so much.

It is very common to want money without doing the work for it but that is impossible, thank goodness. You wouldn't want a world in which those who don't work for something still get it or those who take business risks don't get rewarded.

Even if the 15-year-old singing star seems too young to be so good, what you don't know is that she has probably been singing every day since she was five, possibly with a vocal coach. That's 10 years to be an "overnight" success. We all want success today but it only comes to those who are willing to start small, with no exceptions, and put in the time to make it big.

It may seem that many people get rewarded for doing very little but if you investigate, their success isn't a mystery. The "energy in" and "energy out" model is very precise. Even those who inherit wealth still have to be highly educated and work hard to retain that wealth.

Those who take money without earning it, such as by stealing or embezzling, may have money in the short term but not in the long term. They haven't learned how to earn for themselves and all the while they spend the unearned money unwisely because they think the supply will always be there.

## The Dangers of Unearned Money

If you get good karma by helping your community, you can see why unearned money such as an inheritance might be the worst thing to happen to you. It may mean that you stop helping the community and stop your growth. When you wish for large sums of money such as a lottery win that you haven't earned, you are really wishing to opt out of helping your community and to follow your own interests while others work. We all think, "Not me. I will donate money to the homeless. I will give my friends money so they can go to school. I will hire my friends to work for me."

Unless you are wise beyond your years, however, you will not contribute to the community but only take from it. You will be telling your community, "I don't want to give. I just want to take. I want someone to build me a house, someone to build me a pool, someone to clean my house, cook my food and entertain me." You are providing jobs but not working yourself.

There is work to be done in the neighbourhood but it is unlikely you will spend the time to educate yourself and help people by being a doctor, dentist, veterinarian, electrician, civil servant, police officer, accountant, teacher, writer, chemist, architect, carpenter or cook. So how exactly will you be contributing? You will probably not be getting up early five days a week and working hard for eight hours. This is the problem.

Parents in wealthy families have the difficult task of instilling the value of money and hard work in their children, though their family has more than enough money to live on. Healthy parenting in these families involves making sure the child is well educated and still works hard to contribute to the community in any way possible. The alternative is that the children risk becoming idle, getting pulled into drug and alcohol abuse, and losing all their money.

Getting a legal or divorce settlement larger than one is entitled to can be very dangerous. I'm not talking about legitimate settlements that are redressing a wrong or replacing lost work time from an accident or from raising children. I'm talking about revenge money that lawyers may seek for a client. This money might damage the person receiving it if s/he takes money s/he didn't earn. A person who doesn't know the value of the money may waste it on negative uses, such as drugs and alcohol, and stop contributing to the community. You do not want money you have not earned.

Gambling will never pay because no work is being done. The community will not pay you to sit at the blackjack table for three hours but the community will gladly pay you to help build a building, bridge or road for three hours. I don't think everyone fully understands that with gambling you never win. Never! It's simple math. Unless you win one of the one-in-a-million jackpots, the house eventually wins. Even if you win some at the beginning, over a short time of gambling you will give all the money back. When you see someone win $6,000, it is very likely he has already spent at least $10,000.

Again, lack of self-love and wanting to feel special is the culprit that causes many of us to gamble. Unless you realize it's just for fun and you know you will lose, you really want to believe you are out of the ordinary and that there is a shortcut to wealth for the chosen few. But this is not true. The hotels are doing the work in this case, not the gambler. The casinos are providing entertainment. We pray and hope that God or the universe thinks we are special and can override the odds and let us win, but we are always disappointed. The chronic gambler feels that no one knows he exists and that a big win would prove he is special. The occasional win makes him feel momentarily exceptional and worthy. Chronic gamblers often talk about the "rush" and the "high" they get when gambling. They sound like substance abusers. It's not that the person is not worthy and deserving of wealth, but getting money without giving to the community cannot be done. It's impossible.

Try winning at the horse track when they skim 25% right off the top. Even playing Texas Hold'em, where a great deal of skill is involved, you are usually playing with players of similar skill and the house will slowly sneak away your money. You will blame it on a bad beat or wonder how you still are broke when you have been playing so well.

With lottery tickets, we've all been there. We love the feeling of hope we get from fantasizing about what we would do with the money if we won. We would finally feel worthy because of all the money that could buy happiness. But why not love yourself and be happy today? If you're waiting for a lottery win, you are spending money unwisely and putting off genuine ventures to earn money. We love the hope of winning but it is a false hope. The odds are about one in 12 million to win a major jackpot. Don't be too hard on yourself when you don't win because there are 11,999,999 other people who lost alongside you. And even if you did win it is very common for people to spend "easy" money just as fast as it is made and they are broke again in no time.

Overcoming the almost insurmountable odds to win a substantial lottery, a slot machine jackpot, a major poker tournament, or receiving a large inheritance or legal settlement is only a benefit to your life if the money is valued. Realizing that money is really just a certificate of exchange for hard work done in the past will help you to retain it and possibly create even more wealth through hard work. The money could be used, for example, to increase housing if you bought or developed real estate, or for seed money to help you build a business. It could be used to pay for your education or it could allow you more time to spend with your children or care for elderly parents.

Someone older who has worked hard all his or her life and inherits a large sum or wins the lottery usually spends the money very differently from someone who has not worked very long. Older people may buy a house and car and travel but they will value and take good care of these purchases. They may also help other family members increase their wealth by paying for their education. They may work less in the work force but use their extra time to volunteer in their community and spend more time helping at home with their family.

A person who does not know the value of work, however, will probably spend the money on the instant gratification provided by drugs, alcohol and sex. They may use the money to feel better about themselves by "buying" friends. This is why so many young movie stars, musicians or any young people who receive large amounts of money get into trouble. They may initially earn great karma for their acting and entertaining, but when they stop working or are no longer called on to work and if that career was all they knew, they start having problems. They don't know how else to give but they still want to receive, or they feel it beneath them to work any other way and eventually feel useless. Instead of helping the community with their free time, they spend it on destructive behaviours such as partying with drugs and alcohol. There's nothing wrong with partying responsibly but when it becomes an empty way to feel better about yourself and you abuse drugs and alcohol, then it's a problem.

Having lots of money makes it too easy to choose quick fixes such as drugs to solve major human issues. Instead, we should be grateful we have human issues to tackle, as it makes us become more complex people. Successful young actors and musicians are the ones who continue to work hard in the movie or music business or in some other capacity, such as educating themselves, dedicating themselves to the hard work of raising a family or becoming spokespersons for causes of importance to them. Others get stuck in the past and stop contributing.

*As a rock star, I have two instincts. I want to have fun, and I want to change the world.*
*I have a chance to do both.*
—Bono

## Business Wealth

Successful business owners have long known about karma and giving. There is a direct relationship between how much effort you put into your business, how well you treat your customers and employees, and the long-term success of your business. Businesses that provide great customer service will get repeat customers. Businesses that work hard to keep a clean store or office make it enjoyable to come back to visit.

I recently purchased a cinnamon bun from a small bakery. Instead of giving me one of the freshly baked ones sitting there, he gave me a day-old one. It was actually still frozen inside because it really was from an old batch. He didn't give me a choice and when I drove away and bit into that semi-frozen cinnamon bun instead of a freshly baked one, I vowed never to go back. He saved about 25 cents in food costs and lost a customer forever.

Treating your employees well and having a great working environment will help you retain employees and encourage them to work harder for you. Because your employees will feel better about their work and more loyal to your business, they will be less likely to steal and they will help keep customers because they treat the business as their own.

Many successful business owners volunteer their time and services to the community, which builds on their good karma and the success of their business. The community picks up on their positive energy and gives right back by patronizing that business when they can.

Working hard at your business is probably a guarantee of success but why do some businesses fail when they seem to be doing everything right? The business must have stopped creating energy. It is not providing anything that the community needs. You can work 20 hours a day trying to sell typewriters but if this product is of no value to the community when computers and tablets exist, then your business will fail. You can have the cleanest, best decorated store with the nicest, kindest, most helpful staff but if the product is outdated, the food in the restaurant is not what the locals like or it's very inconvenient to get to your business, then it will probably fail.

A reduction of interest in a product can greatly affect a mining or factory town if they provide the material or make the product. Should the government subsidize a mining town to keep mining a mineral that is no longer needed or subsidize the typewriter factory and force the community to keep using typewriters to keep the factory open? Of course not. But a government subsidy to help the company or workers change technologies might be a solution. If the town is not diversified and workers cannot easily transfer into other industries, many of them will have to move on to find work.

## Why are Some Countries Wealthier than Others?

Economic wealth comes from work being done by a diverse, educated workforce and running at high efficiency and with low corruption. The more educated and skilled the person is, and the more complex the machines the worker uses, the more work can be done. The more diverse the community that has a system to educate engineers, doctors, electricians, plumbers, mechanics, technicians, builders, accountants, bankers and leaders, the more wealth they will have.

The wealthier countries will always be the ones with the top engineers and skilled workers who can build tunnels through mountains, put satellites into orbit, build skyscrapers, dams, bridges, oil refineries, manufacturing plants, enormous ships and high-speed trains. It is not surprising that these companies or countries create wealth with their long-term planning and expertise. Just think of the work difference of one person carrying a four-kilogram load of coal in a bucket down a rocky path for one kilometre compared to one train conductor driving a 30-car train with thousands of kilograms of coal for 500 kilometres. The work difference is stupendous.

The hardest thing for an economist to explain to the general public is that the reduction of jobs in one area can increase wealth for the community because workers are forced to move into other more efficient or productive areas of the workforce. Over the years, you will need to adapt in the workforce. Job losses cannot be taken personally. An example of this principle is the introduction of computers. Instead of a bank or office using 10 employees to do the accounting by hand, let's say they now only need two employees doing the same work with a computer. The other eight employees can now work elsewhere in the bank or in the community. Just think how much work those eight employees can do elsewhere over the next 30 years. As the computer increases in processing capability, those using them may be doing over 1000 times the original workload. Multiply that over the general work force and you can see the community becoming very wealthy because of more work being done.

You can see why some communities are poor when they get this reversed and have 20 people doing the work of one. They may have 20 street vendors selling the same type of shoes when one store will do. They may have 20 people digging with hand shovels instead of having the capital or training to have one person using a large backhoe. The 20 people share the miniscule profits instead of one person getting reasonable pay. If one can do the work of 20 by using a machine, now the other 19 can now work elsewhere to create wealth for themselves and the community.

The other economic principle that is difficult to explain is that work is infinite. There will always be work. Just like the infinite number of applications for computers and phones, there are infinite ways to make changes to your houses and buildings. There is an infinite amount of technology to be discovered. There are endless ways to change the way we grow and cook food. It's the transition from one technology to the next that can initially be painful and leave some people temporarily out of work as they adapt. The work is still being done, although probably by a machine. The community is still gaining wealth but the distribution of who is getting paid for doing the work may be a problem.

The natural business cycle of supply and demand can be frustrating for employees. One year everyone wants the new type of TV and your TV factory is giving you 60 hours of work a week. The next year nearly everyone has the new technology and your factory does not need you anymore. It is not the fault of the government or the political system but the basic laws of supply and demand in play. All we can do as a community with a healthy continual transition in the workforce is to cover for each other when times are tough and to provide education for job transition.

Corruption is a huge wealth destroyer because the laws of right and wrong are not observed. Businesses and the government make decisions based on influence rather than intelligence, resulting in poorer decision-making. Greed takes over and those in charge get involved in taking without giving back. The system breaks down because no one wants to do business when the natural laws are not followed. Why put in all the work and risk to set up or expand a business if others will take from you or have an unfair advantage? Eventually the system, the company or the country breaks down, because there is more taking than giving.

Some of the poorest communities in the world are victims to those at the top. The ones at the top collect money without doing work and this eliminates any incentive for others to work honestly because their earnings will just be siphoned away through embezzlement and bribes. Why spend hours working to build up your business if it's only going to be extorted away?

How does one get rid of corruption if everyone is involved in it? The first thing to remember is that just because others are doing it, it doesn't make it okay for you to do it. If you are taking bribes and stealing from your job, by the rules of karma you are hurting yourself first. You initially get the extra money but it is an illusion and in the long run you will suffer. That dishonest stream of money will not be there forever and it will prevent you from diversifying and increasing your business or your skill set. The dishonest work may affect your relationship with friends and family and you may be caught and fined or put in jail.

How many political officials do we have to see crying in front of the camera or lying about taking bribes? How many times do we have to see the effects it has on their family or watch them being sent off to jail? Learn about karma before you go into politics.

Businesses and governments can't flourish if bribes and threats are part of the business process, because the system will eventually break down. This is where the media and lawyers can be beneficial by exposing dishonesty. Governments without the watchdog of an open media or fair laws may continue to act dishonestly and be susceptible to corruption.

How do you go against dishonesty if everyone in your boardroom, company, job site, government or police force is acting dishonestly? All you can do is stop yourself first. Show others the way and support any action you can to stop corruption. Don't get tempted by short-term gains. In the long term you will be worse off. Initially, you will face some opposition to your choice but eventually you will get respect from others as they see your life become more fulfilling than theirs. Your family life will be much more successful because you come home to a family that respects you after an honest day's work. At work, you become the honest one and then the trusted one and you become more valuable. Your opinions are valued because they are based on selflessness and honesty. Even if you are fired or pressured out of your position, at least you are away from accumulating negative energy and your life will not dissolve away like theirs.

## Case Study

A cement worker gets the contract for making $1 million worth of sidewalks for the city. He bribed the person in charge to learn what bids were coming in so he could underbid everyone else. Instead of building all the sidewalks he promised, he only makes a few and pockets the money, sharing it with the person at city hall who gave him the contract. He has made a lot of money with minimal work but he is now dependent on this corruption for his income for the next 30 years of his life. If the person at city hall gets fired, the contractor no longer has new contracts. Instead of building all the sidewalks and investing profits in more trucks and equipment for his company, he spends the money lavishly on himself and to impress his friends. He has not learned how to increase his business because he is reliant on easy money. No one else wants to hire him for his work because they hear rumours that he is dishonest, so his business fails. He eventually loses everything, including his wife and kids. The city that allowed this corruption to begin with does not have the sidewalks they were initially promised. Everyone loses.

What a different world it would be if the person who honestly got the contract does excellent work, and then with a positive recommendation from the city, gets even more work.

## Prisons and the Military as Energy or Money Drains for a Community

Imagine 40 people living together on an island. Just as in your community, these people have to rely on each other and share the workload. Ten people cannot contribute much because two are elderly and the other eight are young children. Of the remaining adults, six are in charge of the elderly and childcare. One adult is violent and has to be locked up. One adult is in charge of looking after the violent inmate and one is in charge of policing the community. Two people are in charge of defending against possible attacks from neighbouring islands, so they spend the day building defensive weapons and structures. Four people are in charge of the crops and livestock. Five people are in charge of cooking and the delivery of food and 10 are in charge of buildings and maintenance, transportation, entertainment and miscellaneous.

Multiply each group by 50,000 and in a fictitious city of two million you have:

400,000 children,

100,000 elderly,

300,000 in charge of childcare and elderly,

50,000 in the prison system,

100,000 in the police force or prison guards,

100,000 in the military,

200,000 farmers,

250,000 people in charge of cooking and the delivery of food

400,000 in charge of building and maintenance, transportation, entertainment and miscellaneous

This may not be exactly how your neighbourhood shares the workload but this scenario is to show how much of the community energy is used just for crime control and the military. Having to spend large amounts of money on the policing and protection of your community or country is costly to the economy because these workers are out of the general workforce. Instead, these workers could be in helping out with childcare, food, shelter, transportation or entertainment of the city.

Criminals are extremely costly to society because not only are they out of the workforce but they need workers to look after them. Ideally, you should be working towards having fewer criminals, with a small police force and small military, so that more labour.goes into building wealth for the community.

## The Importance of Infrastructure

If the community has a strong infrastructure of roads, transportation, communication systems, electricity, fresh water, sewer systems, an honest police force and court system, and an education system, then the community runs itself — it has everything it needs to exchange goods and services. Then the farms, businesses, manufacturers and the families can function. Those who are healthy can look after themselves and help others who cannot. If the infrastructure breaks down, it is harder to do business. As the infrastructure increases, it becomes easier to do business.

Infrastructure is important for a community because it allows the community to look after itself and earn its own energy instead of relying on others. If the community or country relies on outside donations of other people's energy, then they have the illusion that things are fine and they won't make any changes. They may increase their family size even though the income coming in is finite. They then become dependent on donations because they don't have their own stream of income and work.

Education is one of the building blocks of infrastructure because it helps citizens become trained to support their community with their various skills and talents. They will be able to look after themselves, treat each other fairly and learn to live a healthy life.

# STEP 9:
## APPRECIATE PRESSURE

One of the easiest ways to get ahead in life is to move out of your parents' house when you are done school. It will force you to work more hours and survive on your own. If you're saving money and going to school, that's different but you will not usually succeed unless you feel pressure. You may just do the minimum to survive because there is no pressure to increase your worth.

The parents' choice to allow their kids to stay at home too long can be negative and cause dependency. The financial pressure is not there and the young adult does not have the incentive to push himself to get more education or a better job or to take risks in the outside world so he will not mature as fast. The young person may miss out on fulfilling relationships with others, have poorer job prospects and in general contribute less to the community.

When I went to university I was single. After changing majors a few times, I finally got a Bachelor of Education degree. It took seven years instead of the traditional five years. A fellow classmate finished his degree in three. He was a young father and he couldn't afford the luxury of taking his time. He had bills to pay. He got special permission to take an extra class each semester and he took extra classes during summer school. He was in the work force teaching four years earlier than I was. The pressure of having a family really motivated him.

Most of us need pressure to get things done. If others take away your pressure by giving you money, they may be harming you. The basic rule of giving is if you help a person become independent, you are helping; if your actions encourage dependency, you are harming. This is why you may not always be helping someone when you give her something for nothing. An example of this is handing over money to a stranger on the street. One stranger buys food with it, which eventually gives him the energy to find a way off the street and repay the karma debt he accumulated. Another person receives the money, buys alcohol with it, gets drunk and just for kicks and anger at a world he doesn't understand, he smashes in a store window. He repeats his behaviour and, since he was given money the day before for panhandling, he does it again the next day and the next, as long as people give him money for doing nothing. You contributed to someone *not* making a change in his life.

That was one action with two very different outcomes. When you give and when you receive you must realize there are consequences. When you are given something, it comes with a repayment plan. It's like a loan. You borrow money from a bank and you have to pay it back with interest. We give and receive so much between each other that we are happy with the arrangement and barely know it exists. There is an equal amount of give and take between us and this is what makes our families and communities vibrant. Those who take more than they give (work) will go into debt because they are paying others to do their work. For example, if you eat out all the time and pay for others to shop and cook your food and do the dishes, then the extra expenses may catch up with you.

When giving to service groups, it's important to realize which services are making someone dependent and which ones are helping someone to be independent. Many users of community services have mental and physical disabilities and may not be able to help, but those who can must always help out. How fair is it for some volunteers to go downtown to a soup kitchen, pay for and cook food for 100 people, collect all that good karma of learning the value of hard work and then go back to their beautiful homes and families and leave people still dependent on others? Let those who can help themselves help too because they also have a human need to contribute and it becomes a win-win situation.

A better solution would be for the volunteers to donate the food and lead the soup kitchen but get those who want to eat it to help out. The users will still get the healthy food and will increase their karma as they learn to cook and give. They will feel better about themselves, feel the joy of giving and contributing, and take a small step toward healthier living. The volunteers still get positive karma because they helped and encouraged.

This karma or energy model works in the jail system as well. If prisoners are left doing nothing in jail, they are not collecting positive karma. They accumulate some karma if they are educating themselves. They have neutral karma if they aren't harming or bothering anyone while in prison. But they seldom develop positive karma until they are working and helping others. The prisons that get the prisoners working and training in different jobs see the most success because prisoners start to learn to give and start repaying what they have taken. The prisoners are given the chance to see the benefits of giving and feeling worthy and they become better people.

Prisoners need to be worked as hard as possible. They have so much negative karma that they need help making it to positive territory. They need to work at least 40 hours a week, just like everyone on the outside and then do all their own cooking and cleaning just like everyone else. Ideally they would be trained in childcare to learn the joy of helping humans instead of taking. All they have known before is how to take, but when they learn the joy and benefits of giving, they can raise their karma level and be transformed.

The only way out of poverty is by giving back to the community, usually in the form of a job. There is no magic formula. You get goods and services either by making money and buying them, trading your labour (I'll build you a chair if you give me two chickens), or making the items or food yourself. What makes it difficult for many people is that they are physically or mentally incapable of working the amount that it takes to live comfortably. The universe asks that you do the best you can do with what you are given. Obviously, if there is something that you can do to increase your health, like eating better and exercising, it is up to you to do it.

You should cover for each other and do each other's work with grace and no regrets if you feel you are not being used. If one of your workmates or family members is injured or disabled or depressed, it does not seem like a chore to help them if they are grateful. Like looking after small children or pets, humans love helping people or animals who cannot help themselves. It's when adults can help themselves and are not grateful that there is resentment.

Giving money blindly to communities (excluding emergency situations such as a flood or an earthquake) is like giving money blindly to anyone and could easily have negative consequences. Communities that become dependent on donations may not change their broken systems. Contributing to a group`s infrastructure and education system so they can help themselves is always a great idea but simply doing their work will take away their pressure to educate themselves and be independent.

## Case Study

Town 1 is given a loan to install a new water system for drinking water. The townspeople value the money they will have to repay and spend it wisely. They shop around for the best deal and learn how to install the system themselves so they can reduce installation costs and so they know how to repair and maintain it. This new skill can now earn them money as they teach new communities.

Town 2 is given the money from an outside agency for the same water system. Those in charge of the money hire some outsiders who promise a kickback, bribe money, to build a water system. Instead of looking around for the best deal and saving some of the money for repairs, they keep the extra money for themselves. After the water system breaks down, they don't know how to fix it and they cannot afford to hire an outsider. They are left with a useless water system. They haven't learned the skill of installing the water system, so they cannot fix it or charge other communities for their services.

This scenario plays out in infinite ways in every community. If you don't have a diversity of skilled workers in your community, you will become dependent on others to do your work or no work gets done. If you know someone will always bail you out, there is no pressure to perform. Being reliant on your family, church or welfare system can be damaging if you don't have the motivator to make money or pay it back. Sometimes those from the humblest beginnings become the wealthiest because of the pressure to look after themselves.

# STEP 10:
## AVOID WAR

*Mankind must put an end to war before*
*war puts an end to mankind.*
—John F. Kennedy

The obvious elements of karma and energy and the craziness of war and conflict is what originally got me thinking about writing a book. War provides the perfect formula for understanding how negative energy goes out and brings negative energy right back. It is so much easier to learn to get along than to spend billions of hours on building war machines and training people to use them so they can kill and maim. War shows what happens when you get false self-esteem by belonging to a group; if you blame others, don't think long term, and are more concerned with your own ego than with the welfare of others.

War after war sees both sides using mostly young males to fight out a conflict that seems necessary at the time but after it is all done, puts two groups in a kill or be killed situation.

All that is left is death, injury and destruction. Wasn't every single past war disastrous? Why do we keep signing up for the next one?

You can have the greatest intentions in the world. You can think you are being a person of character, righteousness and honour, but isn't the other side just thinking the same? Are they justified in harming you? The only true statement is that any fighting will result in death or physical and/or psychological injury (P.T.S.D), such as the regret of killing or injuring another human or seeing it happen. Any change or disagreement in society should come slowly through giving and kindness, not by the use of force.

War is 100% negative energy. It's like a machine that, instead of creating and building the community, destroys and takes resources from the community. It kills and injures people, destroys buildings, and in some cases destroys crops, livestock and infrastructure (bridges, roads, power and water systems). It takes workers who would normally be at home with their families, working in the community, building and improving, and turns them into soldiers and takes them away from home. It converts local production for the community into production of bombs and weapons that destroy other communities.

Of course, those who instigate war may mean well at first. They always think they will win and they hope it is a short-term destruction that wards off a "possible" worse destruction. Whether based on a real or imagined threat, to go to war with another group causes such devastation to humanity that it should never be done. When would it be okay for your city to settle a dispute with a neighbouring city by use of force? Obviously, never under any circumstance. Kindness and cooperation are always the answer. If you use force you are not getting to know the other side and there is almost always a racist element to the conflict.

There have been thousands of wars over the years and we have still not learned that force will never be a way to solve problems. War is probably a million times worse than we could imagine. There is extreme pain and suffering for everyone involved. The injuries, the loss of parents and children and other loved ones, and seeing the cruelty of the human heart that could kill, torture and rape during times of war is unbearable.

Don't use the excuse that you are doing it for your country, religion or your beliefs. The easiest example of this folly is the suicide bomber who believes he or she is doing good. Nothing could be further from the truth. The death and destruction caused by the bomber has only negative consequences, including the loss of the misguided bomber's precious life. To choose to kill and maim others rather than using kindness will always mean your choice is the worst one.

We need a local and world police force but not large-scale-country militaries that seek advantage over others and use intimidation rather than cooperation and kindness. You would never use force on your neighbour to solve a problem, so why should you be allowed to use force on the world stage? Again, the evils of ego and of using the group as part of your identity seem to be the common denominator in getting large numbers of people involved in war. Associating a large part of your identity and worth with your culture, country or religion has artificially increased your confidence as you try to increase the power of your group and tear down opposing groups and beliefs. Once you develop blind loyalty to your group you will be willing to die for it as millions of soldiers have done in the past and continue to do.

Even today we are too closely tied to our culture, religion and country for a sense of self and all too easily join our selected group for war. Not being willing to die for your religion or your homeland does not mean that you are abandoning God or your country. On the contrary, it just means you just want to settle differences with positive instead of negative energy and avoid bloodshed. If you feel compelled to get rid of a group different from your own, then your actions are ego-driven and are not going to end well. The universe is vicious to those who try to solve problems with violence.

I love watching sports and cheering for my favourite team but isn't it odd how loyal you can get about a team who, when it comes down to it, is just trying to move a ball or puck forward into a net or across a goal line? Isn't it odd that you feel better about yourself when your team wins, even though you had nothing to do with it? Why is it that we cheer for our home team and dislike their rivals, yet if these teams were to do a complete trade of players, we would cheer for all the new players? Have you ever played a friendly game of football and immediately bonded with your randomly selected teammates? Have you ever become emotional when a fellow countryman wins a gold medal in the Olympics, even though he or she may have immigrated to your country only a few years ago?

Loyalty and a common bond with others are great for adding excitement to sports but a problem arises when it comes to loyalty in wars. What would happen if I went right up to your face and told you, "Your football team sucks." You would probably want to punch me. The local team has become part of your identity and you are ready to fight to the death to defend it. If that's true, you might be a little too connected to your primal brain (in charge of survival of the group). You can see how gangbangers and other young men, not aware of ego, could kill for the supposed benefit of their group. We see young people on both sides ready to fight because it seems the honourable thing to do.

Most armies are built on a very young base. Countries take advantage of a young person's ideals of loyalty and his need for employment. Many wars are filled with young men and boys who lie about their age, ready to jump into the fight. Every war is the same. Young men, peaceful and innocent one day, are easily whipped into a frenzy of hate and are now loyal and ready to kill. Both sides of a conflict treat the soldiers as heroes for defending something. Both sides think what they are doing is so honourable and necessary that they would give their life for it, but again and again it turns into slaughter. Those remaining are left physically and mentally damaged and susceptible to alcohol and drug abuse and suicide.

Young males don't understand the big picture of life and are being used because of their lack of maturity. Who else but a young man could justify bombing or shooting another human? They can take a bayonet and jam it into another human's heart. They can carpet-bomb and drop napalm on an area that guarantees women and children will lose their lives. They feel no immediate compassion as they torture another and chop off or force others to chop off another man's hands to intimidate the enemy. Only young men could throw poison gas into a trench and know that the enemy soldiers would die a slow painful death. Only males can build and then drop atom bombs on cities, knowing that people are getting their skin burned off.

On both sides of a dispute, the community praises its children's bravery for fighting for their country, but this is ridiculous. It's not honourable to kill to solve a problem. If both sides praise their young soldiers for fighting it out to the death, nothing gets solved. One side will eventually outlast the other but it does not mean their cause was any more just; it just means they had a stronger military or more resources.

We know it's wrong for the other side to teach their soldiers that we are evil and that it's for the greater good that we are being destroyed. But it's wrong for us to think that way about them. If we are not promoting peaceful choices, we are part of the problem.

I would have had to fight against the Russians during the 1980s if "the West" had gone to war against them. I wouldn't have been old enough to know any better and would easily have succumbed to the community's honouring of the soldier. I may be strongly against communism but is fighting the only solution? Would I have thought about what it was like to take another person's life? Would I have thought about the Russians I killed and realized they had sisters and brothers and mothers and fathers who loved them? If I wasn't killed or injured, could I have just gone back to a regular life and gotten married and raised my family as if nothing had happened? Would I be seen as a hero?

*How can I save my little boy from Oppenheimer's deadly toy*
*There is no monopoly in common sense*
*On either side of the political fence*
*We share the same biology*
*Regardless of ideology*
*Believe me when I say to you*
*I hope the Russians love their children too*

—Sting (Russians, 1985)

Belonging to an international military that stops a war that the whole world agrees is wrong may be fine, but belonging to a national military usually means you are in it only for the promotion of your group. Just think of the seemingly average Germans who *ecstatically* followed a creepy Hitler just because he made them feel superior, gave them someone to blame any problems on (mostly the Jews), and offered the German people advantage and dominance over others.

What's stopping us from following a charismatic leader today that promises us advantage over others? Once in a national military how do you opt out if your leader is going to war for revenge, racist issues, or from misinformation? How do you stop a chain of command where you are punished or killed for not killing?

What a political mess we are in, with our heads of state negotiating with other heads of state, threatening use of force over meaningless issues. Why do many continue to follow our leaders to our death? Not one exterior issue is worth fighting for. Only family issues are important. The world is just groups of families working together. Don't let imaginary borders and selfish ideological issues separate us into groups that want to dominate. Groups are the enemy. How dare the elders use you to kill other young people?

Trying to intimidate and use power over others always ends badly. Equality and giving is the answer. Parking your extreme arsenal inside or outside someone's backyard to force their hand may encourage terrorism, as it becomes the only way to fight back when overpowered. One day the locals are friendly and cute little Ewoks; the next day they're viciously snapping the heads off Stormtroopers with a tree branch and a piece of rope.

Look up the number of those killed and injured in past world wars and civil wars and examine the figures; sometimes millions have been killed. Could these wars have been avoided? What were the common denominators that started them?

When we go to war, we are really going to war with ourselves. This is one world. Let's not get swept up in the fear game and hurt one another. Nothing good comes from conflict. Just think of all the wasted time western and eastern countries spend spying on each other, building up their war machines with negative energy, instead of helping each other.

Just think what would have happened if Germany's strong work ethic had gone into helping their neighbours in the past, as today, instead of trying to dominate others during World Wars I and II and getting 50 million people killed. The wars were caused by too much false self-esteem based on identity with the motherland and needing dominance over others to achieve a false greatness.

How much better is it to help each other, even when our differences are great? The enemy isn't the group that looks different from you, has more or less skin pigment or who uses a different book for inspiration. The enemy may be yourself and people in your own community who want to hide behind the group to harm others for their own supposed personal gain. They push through their personal agendas to justify their sense of existence and keep the status quo.

It's ironic that the countries with the largest militaries are the ones least likely to be invaded, and not just because of their strong armies. Most of these countries have huge territories and complex cities with millions of people to administrate. Countries that have a large military must base their ideas on fear and/or wanting to use force instead of cooperation to settle issues.

From an economist's point of view, war is extremely expensive. It uses members of the workforce to plan strategies and machines of destruction, instead of strategies and machines to make the world a better and more liveable place. It looks as though the war machine creates jobs but it really just extracts resources and tax dollars from around the country and isolates them in a few locations. Some technological breakthroughs do take place that can benefit the community, but at great expense. Money that could be used for the infrastructure of hospitals, schools or transportation instead gets sent to isolated areas around the country to be used for war machines and munitions.

Then there is the future cost of the expensive medical system, pensions, and payments that could have been used in other ways in the community instead of the hours of rehabilitation time for the soldier after being subjected to such wasteful fighting.

Instead of retaliation, let the violent people implode on themselves, as eventually everyone around them sees their violent energy as wrong and justice will prevail.. Every reason for conflict may be different but every call to action has the precise elements of karma. You will *always* get violence back.

It is very hard to go against the angry mob that wants retaliation and wants to destroy others. It is easier and perhaps in the short term, safer, to comply with the violent group. You may feel as though you are betraying your country or religion. Even leaders of the countries who don't want to respond with violence get pressured into it so they don't seem weak. Why do their approval ratings go up when they act tough? We must all take responsibility.

## Possible Methods to End War

1. Think long term. Develop an understanding of karma and of how every bit of destruction you send your enemy's way comes right back on yourself. War is one area where karma seems to be precise. One side fires 500 units of hate and fear at the enemy, and 500 units of hate and fear come right back. Of course, in the awfulness of war the exchanges are all the more concrete, resulting in death, injury and psychological damage. Send in armies of kindness rather than armies of killing. Stop the cycle.

2. Raise the age of soldiers. Countries should not be allowed to take advantage of the younger person's

patriotism and need of a job. Add in the younger primal brain that is ready to kill for the tribe and each side has its young people believing that what they are doing is honourable, but it's not necessarily so. Young people may not see the big picture and be fighting for the wrong reasons. Do everything you can to keep young males from having too much responsibility in your community. See the devastation caused by young male drug lords and young policeman taking bribes in impoverished communities. Help young men contribute to the group in healthy age-appropriate jobs and not just stick them in jail after they fail.

3. Develop an understanding that the use of force immediately shows your ideals to be invalid. Peaceful methods are the only valid way to settle conflict. If you think your country or culture or religion is worth dying for, then it is *not* worth fighting for, since it is a country or culture or religion of hate and violence.

4. Decrease war budgets and use energy in conflict prevention. It is too easy to go to war if you already have a huge war machine idling on standby. It's too easy for a leader, giddy with power, to make a phone call to attack. Put money into education about the devastation of war instead. Increase the number of student exchanges and travel between countries. Encourage more political energy and institutions to work towards peace and prevention rather than conflict. Encourage and support more women in the administrative and negotiating processes of our countries. Many countries are way too male dominated to function peacefully. Male-dominated countries are almost always the most violent. Prevention is millions of times cheaper than war and no one gets hurt.

5. Be aware of the group. Start to see the world as groups of families and cities rather than as countries. Give more political decisions to families and cities than to national ethnic or religious groups. Those who want a strong national group seek dominance over others. Stop trying to get power from the group and get it from yourself. People need to feel empowered to create their own happiness rather than blaming or hiding behind the power of the group or country or leader for their sense of worth. Millions of people live in harmony in big cities, right now, by respecting each other's differences without needing to belong to a group.

   In the future, when advanced travel options will have you working in Paris in the morning, Beijing in the afternoon and vacationing in Brazil on the weekend, there will be no borders. You will not be able to hide behind your group or tribe for false self-esteem. You will be judged on how you treat others, how well you work, for your advancement in society.

6. Don't retaliate. How do you not retaliate when the other side has killed people in your community? The initial reaction is to fight back and make them pay immediately for what they have done but of course that will only make things worse. Just like fighting a bully, it only justifies their action and causes more violence. If you show your positive energy, the other side will eventually see their ugliness and will have to stop. Everyone around them will demand it. Peaceful action will take us down the healthiest long-term path.

Could you imagine our world today if there were never any wars but only peacetime prosperity? Could you imagine all units of work going to civilian life rather than destruction? There would be no death, injuries or pollution from the giant machines of war and no psychological damage from those who have participated in and witnessed the worst of humankind.

*Imagine there's no countries*
*It isn't hard to do*
*Nothing to kill or die for*
—John Lennon (Imagine, 1971)

Atomic weapons have to be eliminated from all countries. This is humanity at its most insane. I know it's meant to be a deterrent but it actually increases the threat as more and more countries seek the ultimate weapon. All countries should band together to prevent any country from having such weapons. Only when there are no atomic weapons will the chance of atomic annihilation dissipate.

To be a part of the solution, young people should not contribute to the war machine in any way. It is very hard to stand up to the violent group that uses force over kindness but peaceful measures are the only long-term solution. It is difficult to refuse a well-paying job building, selling or using weapons but you have to think long term to stop this insanity. If an industrialist pushed for war or a military build-up so he could profit, we would call him psychotic. But isn't a worker who wants increased military spending so he can have a job doing just the same? It will cost you more in the long run. It's not worth the cost of mourning for lost loved ones and all the extra taxes to pay for the war machines and the rehabilitation of the war wounded.

Instead of going in a warship to stop a conflict, consider a peace ship. Force will only collect negative energy. Being sent in a peace ship that is stocked with supplies for building schools, increasing agriculture and supporting infrastructure is the only way to raise positive energy and the only way to come back alive and a better person.

# STEP 11:
## HELP INCREASE MALE KARMA

Men have come a long way but still most of the negative karma in the world comes from men and usually young men. Young men tend to settle conflict by fighting, bullying, filling the prisons, backing up the courts and being foot soldiers and leaders of gangs. Men are the most likely gender to be paedophiles and arsonists, be cruel to animals, create computer viruses, commit identity theft and be the most reckless drivers by speeding or drinking and driving. Young men are the ones willing to fight in wars, to torture, sell and use drugs, steal, kidnap, enslave, rob, embezzle, vandalize or rape, oppress and abuse women. What has happened?

Is it our genes or excess testosterone? Is it because boys are not given enough love and attention, or too much, or raised to be aggressive and competitive? Is it because they don't know how to handle disappointment and anger or the way they feel powerless in the community?

For some reason, some young males have lost the connection between what the community and past communities has done for them and yet they still want to take without giving back. It may be because of a world of specialization of labour, where there aren't many areas where young males can help until they are skilled and older, but we still let them dominate in gangs, the military, the police and in relationships. They are given way too much responsibility before they have the maturity to choose peaceful avenues. These young men are seldom taught to help with childcare, care for the elderly or help others with disabilities. They are encouraged to take up sports and to be competitive in the world and in getting a mate. They are encouraged to make money to be a good provider for the family but not necessarily for the good of the world. To add to all this responsibility, they are at their optimum sex drive.

Sex is a huge motivator for positive or negative male behaviour. For whatever reason, sex occupies much of the male's brain and money is seen as a direct way to impress, to feel value, get respected and of course help with getting more sex. With this comes a pressure to come by money quickly and attempt shortcuts. Unfortunately, wealth takes time and all you can do is be a great human being first and success will follow.

Let's examine three ways young men get into the trap of unhealthy violent behaviour.

## 1. Young men tend to look up to older men who are aggressive and violent because they are under the illusion that these men get wealth and girlfriends without having to do very much work.

Young men think other men and women will look up to them if they are dominating, strong and aggressive, but this isn't necessarily true. Now that you understand karma, you know that this negative behaviour has only short-term positive results with long-term heartache. Dominating a woman prevents you from having a healthy relationship with her. Violence towards others affects your relationships because eventually nobody wants to be around you and everyone will find a way to exit your life. Resorting to violence to get what you want is only short term and will cause others as well as yourself to hate you. You may attempt to cover up this disappointment by using drugs and alcohol.

You may need to stick up for yourself but don't do it at the expense of others. If you're taught at home to take instead of give, or fight instead of compromise, you will have negative energy. Whole neighbourhoods are ruined by this mentality. These areas get so rundown and violent that no one wants to shop or open up a business there. The areas deteriorate and become slums. The healthiest way to get respect and build your community is by giving, not by flashing a gun.

## 2. Men who are desperate to try to impress others, particularly a mate, may resort to negative behaviour.

Young men get sucked into negative behaviour because they desperately want to impress others, particularly a potential mate, but the rules of giving and receiving need to be acknowledged. You can't steal, intimidate, lie, or show off to impress others or you are going to get hurt, killed or incarcerated. The question shouldn't be, "What does it take to be a man?" but "What does it take to be a healthy human being?"

For some reason we call unhealthy human behaviour "manly." We look up to those who think short term and bully, beat up and take from others. For some reason some of us strive to be manly by beating up other men, dominating our girlfriend or wife, jumping over 10 buses with a motorcycle or being ruthless in business. It's true that it's mostly men who engage in this behaviour, so in a sense it is "manly" but not healthy. It's true that women see men who take risks as good providers but they have to be risks that don't hurt anyone. Don't look up to these troubled souls who are trying to impress others by living dangerously, because they are in for a lot of mental and physical hurt in the future. They will never have healthy relationships and will spend a lot of time in hospital or in jail.

Being a man, you should strive to be strong, a good leader or someone who takes healthy risks but these are also characteristics of a healthy human. If you use your physical strength to dominate others, you hurt yourself most. No one will want to be around you. Having healthy, equal relationships with others is where most joy comes from.

Let's be honest. The dominant men seem to have more money and get the most attractive partner. This may be partly true but much of this "success" is short term, and what kind of partner did they attract? If a woman values dominance and taking from others then she isn't worth fighting over. Only the unhealthiest of women will be attracted to men who are aggressive, rather than giving and who make short-term money by taking from others. Their relationship is dysfunctional. Who's got lower karma in the Hells Angels or the Mafia: the men or the women?

Young women attracted to men in the drug trade are initially interested in them because of what looks like a life of easy money and privilege. They risk getting addicted to drugs, being killed in retaliation by competitors and are not in a situation to advance themselves through hard work or schooling.

For any man who gets wealthy from deceiving, stealing, selling drugs and other negative ways, the wealth will be short lived and so will the relationships that come with it. It must be very painful to have a lot of money for a short while and then to end up poor or in jail, addicted to drugs or alcohol, and in dysfunctional relationships that are only there while the money lasts. On the other hand, life must be quite joyful for those who slowly build their wealth by giving to the community. They keep their wealth and have healthy functional and honest relationships.

The wealthy man who may be attractive to the opposite sex has earned his appeal if he developed it honestly. He is bound by the rules of wealth and has had to work hard by educating himself, taking healthy risks and working long hours. His drive and his bank account may make him attractive but the couple still has to find a healthy, balanced give-and-receive relationship that is not based on a power struggle over money.

Men need to learn that you earn a relationship. You do not selfishly take. You do not take sex from someone by abusing, raping or taking advantage of a situation to get sex. Kindness and giving is the only way towards a healthy relationship. See the woman's point of view. This is a time to try to understand the opposite sex because women have different values and priorities, particularly because they can have babies and because men are physically stronger. Unfortunately there are too many men abusing women. There are far too many women in need of abuse shelters after they finally realize they must leave a dominating man who wants to control and hurt them.

*3. Men who compare themselves to their successful elders may be overwhelmed by how long it takes to accumulate wealth and healthy relationships and may resort to short-term negative behaviour in an attempt to bypass the hard work that is necessary.*

Some young men are overwhelmed by how long it takes to acquire wealth and this desperation causes them to become destructive, as they lash out at the apparently closed system. Young men will look for "easy" money and look for any shortcut such as gambling to compress the long journey, but it never works. I'll be honest with you, the journey to accumulate wealth is very long but there is no other way. It takes years. Follow any elder's career and you'll see that there are no shortcuts to gaining wealth and good relationships. It takes years and years of educating yourself, taking chances and working hard. That's why you have to live in the present and enjoy the process.

You see older men with a house, fancy car, a girlfriend or wife and a healthy family life and you want it now. Most young people don't realize that their elders spent years going to school and university and years of taking all sorts of low-paying jobs before climbing up the job ladder. They worked hard raising a family and worked on their relationship with their spouse. I sometimes get envious when I see retired men relaxing on the golf course when I know I have at least 15 more years of working and contributing before I can afford to go golfing with any regularity.

As a young person, you will eventually get your turn to contribute and receive the benefits that come from giving to society but it takes time. A giant building started as an empty lot but after thousands of hours of design as well as all the work that goes into the building materials and construction, it becomes a building. A movie starts out with an idea but after thousands of hours spent on writing, producing, making the movie, editing the movie and distributing it, it gets done. Everything is overwhelming at first, but with effort it will happen.

One day, machines may do nearly everything for us but, as we are finding out, the more machines that do our work and the more we have, the more we want. We will never be happy unless we enjoy the *process* of living and growing today. Doesn't it feel better to have earned something instead of getting it handed to you? Could you be a rock star if you hadn't put in the hours of practising, writing and travelling? Doesn't winning a sport championship make you cry with joy, not just because you won, but because of all the effort you put in over the years to get you to that place of victory? Don't you want to earn your business or work your way to the top of the business world, instead of having it handed to you? Or, if you inherit a business, don't you want to be educated and work as hard as your ancestors to ensure that the business prospers?

Wealth can be a bit of an illusion anyway. The more things you have, the more things you need to maintain. Those with three houses have to maintain three houses. You can only eat so much food. You can only sleep in one bed. Everything costs more for the wealthy: their food, their houses, their cars, the schooling for their children and even their alcohol. Let those who need to impress pay hundreds of dollars for a bottle of wine or champagne. Let them pay $80,000 for a car that is really not much better than a $20,000 vehicle. Let them pay millions for an old vase or painting or thousands for shiny rocks that come out of the ground. They may even be forced to go to the opera. Work on being a great human with great relationships, and any wealth — and not necessarily financial wealth — will come naturally.

## Ways to Increase Male Karma

The best way to increase male karma is by being a great role model and/or father. Men will have low karma if they neglect their parenting responsibilities. Men are often the first to leave the family when a marriage or a relationship dissolves. Single mothers usually get the blame for a child not reaching his or her full potential, yet they are usually the ones sticking it out with their child. It is the man who is absent. Helping to raise a child is one of the strongest ways to get great karma for anybody, especially a father. If you are stuck and looking for meaning in life, why not help raise your own child? It shouldn't be seen as punishment or babysitting.

Helping others who cannot help themselves, particularly your own child, can only be a positive experience. If a couple are separated, they have to get over their differences and realize the advantages of having another parent's help, and the child benefits too. The parents who do not help miss out on the experience of the true meaning of life, selfless giving, and gaining positive karma. If they do not help, they may end up chasing false meanings of life by abusing sex, drugs, alcohol and money, and will have children that resent them.

How many children of families with poor (or no) father figures have socializing issues and feelings of abandonment? How many motorcycle and other gangs are filled with lost men, unsure of their place in the world? Their desperate need for belonging and the acceptance of other men in the gang has them doing awful things to the community.

Building up good karma takes time but it will take you much longer if you are in jail or not working. Even in low-paying jobs you are contributing and this usually leads to better opportunities. The advantage of a low-paying job experience is that it forces you to go back to school and educate yourself or to work harder to succeed. Everyone started with awful jobs but it teaches you the value of hard work. I probably wouldn't have gone to university if I'd landed a well-paying job right out of high school.

People of all ages, especially young people, need to understand and embrace the laws of karma and accumulate good energy instead of bad. This is a great time to live in the present, realize all the good things you have, and not rush into the future. You should be jealous of no one. The wealth of men who are older than you is all very well, but it comes with responsibilities that you don't need yet. You don't need the long hours of business and dealing with lawyers and bankers. You don't need the stress of mortgage and car loan payments. You don't need the stress of raising a family and the long hours of childcare. You have your health, your friends and a magnificent period of few responsibilities, so enjoy it. Everything comes with a trade-off, so don't feel jealous of older people's wealth. Wealth will come when you're ready for all the responsibilities that come with it. When the time comes and you are an elder, you will not want to see younger men stealing from you, fighting, abusing drugs and alcohol and not contributing to the community that you have helped to build.

# STEP 12:

## UNDERSTAND DRUGS AND ALCOHOL

When I started writing this book, I had no idea that drugs and alcohol would be a recurring theme. I had no intention of slamming something that I generally thought of as harmful to only a few. I was familiar with some chronic users who took drugs to avoid dealing with past issues, particularly traumatic childhoods of abuse or abandonment, and counselling is needed. What I noticed in almost every section of my book was that it was very common for those who participated in selfish negative behaviour and caused harm to others to cover up the regrets by self-medicating with drugs and alcohol. I believe a moderate use of alcohol can be great for relaxing but it is way overrated.

TV commercials, mostly by breweries, have tricked us into thinking drinking is exciting and glamorous. Beer equals babes and it's unpatriotic not to drink. But this is really one of life's biggest myths. Remember that the brewery's main goal is to sell its product and if it can sell it on the themes of tradition, friendship, sports, and patriotism, it will. And why not? Because young people are easy to influence in this way. I hate to tell you this when you have finally found something that can give you extra confidence, but when you have more than a few drinks, the experience can become a nightmare. The headaches, the throwing up, the injuries and death and the volatile relationships caused by over-drinking just don't make sense. Drinking is a time when you are really selfish to your future self. You have the illusion of a great time at the moment but pain later.

How many fatal accidents are caused by alcohol? How many families are torn apart and how many street people are barely surviving because of their addiction to drugs and alcohol? You hear story after story of the damage done to people because of alcohol. Be very aware. Never mind your messed up life or your childhood — drugs and alcohol will make things worse. We celebrate when people stop drinking, not when they start drinking again.

The world of drugs and alcohol can seem very exciting for a young person. Alcohol helps you loosen the inhibitions that have you have layered on yourself. Alcohol temporarily stops the internal voice you have built up by comparing yourself to others. Drinking means we can stop being so hard on ourselves and say what's really on our mind without worrying about the outcome. It helps us live in the present and puts us in a holding pattern so we don't have to worry about the past or future. Drugs do the same, temporarily making us feel good about ourselves and the world. So what's the problem? The problem is that the alcohol and drug strategy works only while we're using and therefore it is a very short-term solution.

I call alcohol the number one false self-esteem because it is the easiest to use but only works while you are drinking it. You make no behaviour change for long-term growth and alcohol has too many dangerous side effects. Unfortunately, this quick fix is going to be the most tempting for young people and they are the ones most likely to abuse.

We all want a shortcut such as a pill or drink to solve our problems but if no action happens, the results are an illusion. You temporarily feel on top of the world and you're not so hard on yourself, but this will last only as long as you are using and eventually you will have to stop. You aren't living. Your inner strength and inner being are not being observed and you will feel the same about yourself after you finish using. You are no further ahead. You would need to use constantly to feel the effects, like people in an opium den where the users lie like vacant pods, half asleep, hooked up to an artificial life support system, barely living.

What you need to do is get rid of your false self-esteem and comparisons and love yourself authentically. Then you won't have to rely on alcohol. Once you realize that all you have to do is put others first and be kind to others, you start to love yourself and your confidence grows.

Temporarily avoiding life and feeling more relaxed around others may be okay for a few hours on the weekends with friends but not as a lifestyle. Problems are solved by action, not inaction. There can be a positive social aspect to drugs and alcohol but eventually you will find that drugs and alcohol will give mostly negative results. It will certainly be negative if the drugs and alcohol involve you in fighting. It will be negative if you have too much and get sick and throw up or worse, end up in the hospital because of an overdose. It will be negative if you drink and drive and risk hurting yourself or others; negative if it causes you to trip and have a dangerous fall. It will be negative if you miss work and get fired, negative if you cannot afford it. If you make a poor choice hooking up with someone whom you wouldn't have been interested in when you were sober and you get pregnant or contract an STD, the results will be negative. If it affects your ability to have good relationships with others, destroys your body and contributes to a violent drug distribution system, the outcome will be bad.

What happens if you get involved with hard drugs (the nastiest being heroin, cocaine or crystal meth)? People using drugs may do so because of a deep hurt or intergenerational cycle of addiction, where children of addicts are likely to turn to drugs and alcohol. The universe doesn't care about the reason. It only reacts to the negative energy caused by you hurting others.

Using drugs is addictive and it will be very, very difficult to accumulate good karma. Instead, negative karma will result from the pain you cause your family, friends and community. You may have to steal, lie, prostitute yourself or cause property damage to get money for drugs. Drug use is such a downward spiral of negative karma that it's a miracle when anyone gets off them. The addicts have to quit a highly addictive drug and begin the long road to recovery to repair all the damage caused to family, friends and the police and community workers, as well as everyone they stole from and lied to.

Why go down this road? Is your pain so bad that you're willing to replace it with another pain? Put others first, be authentically kind and giving to others, and walls will come down. You will feel such a flood of love that you won't need any drug that gives you a peace that tricks the brain and is only temporary. You don't deserve the pain. Visit any area where drug use is common and see that there is no shortcut to happiness and there will be no way you can see anything positive about the self-centred choice to use drugs. Rehab is usually the only way to get off drugs and even then, the damage to your brain and body can be permanent.

## Marijuana

Marijuana might not be as bad as some other drugs because those who use don't usually harm others. It even has some positive medical benefits relating to stress, glaucoma and the reduction of nausea related to cancer treatments. But it also seems to have many negative effects (particularly to young developing brains), including paranoia, loss of drive and initiative, exposure to a drug culture that could lead to other drugs, and the promotion of the drug trade.

It's an innocent-looking drug that may as well be legalized but it comes with a catch: you might not be causing others harm but you probably won't be collecting very much positive energy either. Using marijuana can put you in a holding pattern of doing very little to help others and just spending a lot of time looking at the back of your hand. You take no positive risks. It can reduce your ability to educate yourself and your motivation to advance your employment and family plans.

## A Drug Producer/Dealer's Karma

What is the karmic effect on the drug producer and dealer? They don't force you to use drugs. I don't think you should ever blame anyone for your actions or for avoiding responsibility, so an addict cannot blame the drug dealers for his or her drug addiction. They were not the ones who put the addict in a vulnerable position or who put the drug in his or her body. The addict made the ultimate choice, but dealers and producers are still acquiring negative energy by supplying the drugs and being a big part of the problem. It should be no surprise that suppliers are left with the negative energy of death and the destruction of their own lives.

The farmer who consciously makes a choice to grow poppies and coca plants that destroy lives will collect negative karma. The opposite would be a farmer who grows plants that feed and nurture the community such as rice, wheat, fruit, and vegetables or any healthy produce. They would collect positive karma with no violence and have a healthy happy family and community.

Communities that contribute to heroin and cocaine production and distribution collect bad karma in the form of violence and disruption of community. It's no coincidence that every country that contributes to the drug trade has a terrible time and that the entire fabric of the community is damaged: locals get addicted, violence occurs over the profits, costs for policing and jails increase. The gun takes on too much value to settle disputes and the valuable tourist trade is lost because people are scared to visit.

Sympathy goes out to the poppy or coca farmer who needs an income to support his family but if farming harmful products gives you bad karma, you will only get violence and poverty in return. The higher cash price for the poppy over wheat becomes an illusion and is not worth it. For every $1 billion injected into the economy from heroin, the economy is missing out on billions more from a healthy infrastructure that does not include drugs. Work is diverted from food products, construction, finance, education and tourism and is replaced by a violent and corrupt infrastructure dominated by smugglers.

You don't want drug smugglers directing your economy through violence and bribery. Everything from politics to religion gets skewed with a drug economy and the basic economy cannot grow. In Afghanistan, the smugglers are violent and have been known to steal and traffic in children for debts unpaid. Back in your home country, you would not want your local farmers growing produce that could be used to destroy humans in other parts of the world.

## Energy Comparison Between Two Farmers

### Wheat Farmer

The wheat farmer grows a plant that is turned into feed for cattle and milled into flour to make bread for human consumption.

The farmer raises cattle to be used as food energy for humans.

The farmer pays taxes and contributes to healthy families and communities.

### Poppy Farmer

The poppy farmer grows a plant that is made into heroin. The drug provides no nutrition. It is addictive and very unhealthy for the user, mentally and physically.

The farmer and local community may end up using the drug and getting all the problems of addiction and violence from the drug trade. Smugglers usually use violence to control the farmer.

Instead of valuable tax dollars that go to the community for schools, roads and health care, much of the profits are used for bribes and corruption that disrupt the community.

A variety of individuals and gangs distribute the drugs and all of them have horrific karma. The harm that drugs cause the community is extensive. Distributors have an awful life of violence, untrusting relationships, paranoia, drug and alcohol abuse, and incarceration. Motorcycle and street gangs and the Mafia are prime examples of how their lifestyles are so negative. We wonder why they live like they do when only bad things happen to them. When will they learn? If they are not killed or put in jail, their bad energy seeps into their relationships with lovers, family and their attempts at legitimate business. Any income is reduced because of the need for money laundering, bribes, security, fines, lawyers and court time.

What is the karma of the person who makes crystal meth? What a psychotically selfish and awful person! This is a terrible, addictive drug that is made with a mix of such toxic chemicals that it damages the body and brain of the user. Depression and other brain chemistry problems are likely with this drug, as is death.

It's surprising that anyone with even a little concern for themselves would try such a drug, if only because of the ingredients. The main ingredient is ephedrine, found in cold medicines. But crystal meth may also contain iodine, Drano, brake fluid, ammonia and many other unbelievably dangerous toxins. I cannot imagine the type of personality that could justify making, distributing or using such an awful mixture. The negative karma must be huge because the drug is so harmful and therefore the producers and distributors of this drug will live an awful life. Mixing dangerous chemicals, the maker risks death and injury from the toxins and possible explosions as well as the regular negative karma of the drug world — violence and, ironically, toxic relationships.

## Smoking

Smoking is something that seems innocent for young people because it has few consequences when you are young. They don't surface until you're older but then they are major. Right now smoking is relatively cheap because if you are still living at home your expenses are minimal. You don't notice the negative health effects because your health is at its optimal level. Eventually, the negatives override the positives as it affects your choice of employment, your relationships, income and of course your health. It would be fine if it weren't addictive and you could use tobacco sparingly but it is very addictive and now all you are is an addict full of excuses for why you smoke. You are stuck with the consequences.

Financially, you will be much poorer than non-smoking adults. You may have already thought of this but let's do the math. If your smoking habit costs you $10 a day, then you will be $3,650 poorer each year. Over 10 years smoking will cost you $36,500 and over 20 years you will be $73,000 poorer. Obviously, this amount will be less if you smoke less and more if you smoke more; this does not take into consideration that cigarettes will probably cost much more in the future.

Your income level could be lower because of other related factors you've never even dreamed of. Non-smokers may discriminate against you in their hiring practices. Non-smokers can't stand smokers and former smokers can't stand smokers, so you may get passed over for jobs that you qualify for. I don't blame them. Besides the disgusting smoke and cigarette butts around a smoker, smokers are always thinking about their next smoke break and are likely to work less.

A smoker may pass up opportunities for advancement because of the particular job's inflexibility in providing a consistent smoking time. A job that goes too long without a smoke break may be out of the question.

In terms of intimate relationships, you are probably limited to other smokers. Only other smokers will put up with the smell of smoke around you and on your clothes and breath. I know I've changed hairdressers in the past because the one I went to smoked. I find it irritating to be greeted by a salesperson or a waiter who has just come in from a smoke break.

Non-smokers will not want to put up with your need to stop and purchase cigarettes and to stop for a smoke break. If a non-smoker is with a smoker, the non-smoker will want the smoking partner to quit and this will put pressure on the relationship.

Kids of smokers want their parents to quit and lose respect for the parents when they don't. Those kids may also lose their good judgment about the negative aspects of smoking because their parents smoke and become more likely to smoke themselves.

The health problems alone should be enough to make smokers quit. The list of health problems associated with smoking isn't limited to lung damage. Smoking affects every organ in your body, including your brain, and about one-third of all cancers are smoking related.[2] You need to pay attention to older smokers and be aware of their health problems, including the possible association between mental illness and smoking, before you start such an addictive habit.

---

2    Tobacco use accounts for at least 30% of all cancer deaths and 87% of lung cancer deaths. (Source: *Cancer Facts & Figures 2013*)

# SUMMARY
## THE PROOF IS ALWAYS
## IN THE RESULTS

I'm a huge fan of this Earth. I think it's perfect. We are able to enjoy a planet that is about four billion years old. It is the perfect distance from the Sun and has matured to be the most amazing place perhaps in the universe. It has given us so much with its different landscapes, climates, minerals, plants and animals, which allow us to eat and build almost anything we can imagine. We have amazing bodies with brains that can solve almost any problem and do almost anything. We're able to love and be loved yet we still complain about everything and fight with each other. We complain that peaches are too fuzzy. The temperature outside is too hot or too cold. We complain that we don't have enough things or enough money or that the world is too confusing. Some are hoping that there is a better afterlife where supposedly you don't have to do anything and everything comes to you. But I do know this is not how this world works. Here everything needs energy to move, to make, to exist. Everything comes from something and if you want it, you have to make it yourself or else trade your work with someone else to get it.

You have to do the best with what you're given and, believe me, it's a lot. Not only do you have a planet and body that is amazing but you have walked into a world where our ancestors have already done trillions of hours of work and where many things are already built and you just have to update and maintain them. Land has been cleared for agriculture, rivers have been diverted for hydro electricity; major transportation systems of roads, bridges, subways and ocean locks for ships are already in place. There is a huge infrastructure of buildings, government, telecommunications and other utilities already in place that means you barely have to lift a finger. All you have to do is your share of the work and be grateful. Just realize how amazing life is and that you are worthy of living here like everyone else. I know you didn't do anything except be born but that's all any of us did. We are all in the same boat and if you don't think you are worthy you will participate in unhealthy behaviour. You will have to put others down, steal, harm others and abuse drugs and alcohol.

If you are grateful and feel worthy of this world then you will want to give to others. This is where your happiness really takes off. When you give to others, by the principle of energy, it comes right back and even better. The people with true joy are the ones who give to others and the ones with true grief are the ones who take.

One easy way to get good karma is by not letting others do your work. This includes not accepting work-credits (money), unless you receive them as a one-time gift. If you live at home don't let your parents clean your room or do your laundry or do anything for you if you can do it yourself. You're letting them have the good karma. They have spent years looking after you and collecting good energy. Now it's your time to start collecting. They have changed your diapers, cooked your food, cleaned the house, paid the bills and given about one-third of their lives and their money to look after you. The world doesn't care who gives or why but it gives back to those who give and you will miss out.

If someone wants to do something nice for you or buy you a gift or give you money, you should graciously accept because you want him to increase his karma. It is a one-time deal and will not make you dependent. We give and receive because we care for each other. Giving is not painful; it actually feels great. Giving and receiving is a win-win situation but if one person is only giving and one is only taking, the balance is thrown off, which can lead to problems of resentment and dependency.

Getting money without earning it almost always causes problems. Perhaps you will not appreciate the money and spend it foolishly because it came so easily. You will not learn how hard it is to make money. Or perhaps the "free" money will prevent you from trying harder at school or in the work-place because there is no pressure to try harder, which affects you in the long term. You may neglect to continue educating yourself and going after more challenging work.

Earning good karma by being kind and giving is taught at the kitchen table. Successful families pass it on to their children by modelling those behaviours. When you watch your parents being honest and hardworking and you see the success in their lives, you learn to do the same. Successful parents talk about the action they take, not the inaction. These parents would feel ashamed if they took something without earning it and would never blame others for their problems.

Children who don't have the greatest role models may see their parents blame others for their misfortunes. Blame will be directed at their bosses, their co-workers, their neighbours, their family members and the government — everywhere but at themselves. Sometimes whole communities and even whole countries blame everyone but themselves and miss out on the connection that "energy out" equals "energy in" and that they are the answer to their problems. Many successful kids learn that they don't want to be inactive blamers like dear old Dad or Mom and can use their childhood as learning experiences in how not to live with low energy.

Travelling around the world can teach you how giving communities prosper and how communities of taking, corruption and blaming suffer. You can see how the different education systems, skill levels, and infrastructure transform each community in different ways. Notice how communities that don't let in others of difference will not get the benefits of new information and they may get stuck in the past.

It's true that you may not have helped build anything, repair anything or contribute to the feeding or sheltering of the community but you are storing karma. Be patient and just do what you can. You will have plenty of time to contribute and until then, we the community will look after you. When you're ready to contribute, it will be at an amazing level. Your parents house and feed you and maybe even pay for your education so that you will not only have the skills for a job that will help you contribute but will become a more rounded person who will make healthier choices and not be a drain on the community.

We tend to look up to those who have taken shortcuts and taken from the community without giving back, such as bank robbers or gangs, because it takes so long to accumulate money karma. However, those who attempt shortcuts that are self-serving and harm the community, like dealing drugs, always get severely punished. In the long run their lives become a disaster as they go in and out of jail and have failed relationships, risk death, injury and drug and alcohol addiction and then financial hardship.

Success comes from putting in thousands of hours of work into whatever you are doing. If you like what you're doing, it makes it much easier to put in the long hours to get good at playing the guitar, skateboarding, painting, building or whatever it may be.

I can tell you that the stove is hot but you need to touch it to prove it to yourself. I can tell you not to drink too much but you may still find yourself puking on your best friend's shoes. You will have to love yourself today in order to prevent yourself from doing something when there are no second chances. There may not be a second chance if you try an addictive drug like heroin. You may not get a second chance if the acid or ecstasy pill scrambles your brain. There may not be a second chance if you kill or injure someone or yourself when you drink and drive.

The only real advice I give to my own kids is to be kind and giving to others and look after their health. If you exercise and eat mainly unprocessed foods your brain will be healthy and it will make great decisions. If you are kind to others you will automatically love yourself. You will not need to put others down and others will be kind back to you. Having joy and happiness right now is that simple. If someone is having a bad day, don't throw fuel on the fire. Instead, help them put the fire out. They will change by being around a great role model like you.

Karma is precise but tomorrow is another day. Everything has a reason. You won't feel envy when you see someone with an expensive house now that you know they have earned it or will be working hard in the future to pay off their mortgage. You will not be tempted to steal because you know that it will make you poorer. You will not sell or abuse drugs and alcohol because you realize the negative karma will cause your life to be worse. You will only accept peaceful solutions instead of war with others or you will be worse off. This is just the way it is. You are in charge.

How do we explain the less tangible ways of karma, such as when we do something that has no immediate consequences? What happens when we throw garbage on the ground, dump poison in the ocean, say unkind words about others, steal movies or music through the Internet or do nothing for our community? What kind of karma accrues for those who build weapons, fight in senseless wars, sell drugs, steal, accept a bribe or lie? The long-term damage to our environment and the long-term damage to the children of war will come back to haunt us. We will be given appropriate consequences for our actions.

Some karma seems mysterious because it comes from past decisions and may take years to materialize but it will take place. It's like planting an apple seed and waiting for years to enjoy apples from the time and energy you initially took to plant the tree. If you do good, goodness will come back to you but you may need patience.

I am not good with helping those getting flooded from a broken dam while the dam still has holes in it. I need to fix the structure first. I would never make a good military medic. I wouldn't want to help fix the wounded until I helped stop the war first or there will just be more bodies to fix. I find it much easier to find peace with my neighbours instead of building a giant wall or building a mega war machine to separate us. I find it easier to teach others to stop following false-esteems and find self-love to get people off of drugs, than use force and prisons. I find it much easier to teach the importance of birth control and the ignorance of some parts of religions, over having thousands of unwanted pregnancies that can lead the family and community to poverty, crime and overpopulation. I find it easier to teach about karma instead of seeing young people self-destructing and ending up in jail.

You can never blame God or the universe because everything has a reason for why it happens. You are not being punished. Diseases have an exact chemistry. Miscarriages and cancer have an exact cause. Whether it is heredity, environment or diet, there is a reason. Thank goodness, because as we figure out the body, doctors can help heal us and we can change our behaviour. Even being killed or injured in a car accident or at the job site is the risk we take driving giant metal speed machines or using dangerous equipment. All we can do is reduce the odds by using these machines responsibly, giving them our full attention when we use them, and not using drugs or alcohol, or a phone while operating them. We can look after our bodies the best way we know and do the best we can with what we are given.

If being kind and giving to others is easy to do and if it makes our lives better, why don't we all do it? It's as though our brains are split in two. Half of our brain thinks we are more important than anyone else and it wants to take without earning. This is usually considered the ego. It means well and can work as a motivator to get us to try harder. However, it makes us overly concerned with ourselves and wanting to take, without feeling concern for others. The ego constantly needs to feel important and special; under extreme circumstances, it can get out of hand. It can be so concerned about what people in the community think that it has led fathers to "mercy kill" daughters when the daughter chooses to marry someone who doesn't match their family or cultural image.

The psychotic ego is one that cares about itself and would not hesitate to steal, rape, abuse a child or kill another for personal satisfaction. The ego part of the brain that wants to impress others can hurt its master if it gets the young man to jump off cliffs, do dangerous stunts, drive at speed or fight to impress.

Even over-emphasis on our personal appearance can have a negative outcome if it leads to eating disorders, unnecessary plastic surgery or spending too much time or money shopping. It's very common for people to think that material things will impress, while all they do is get them into serious debt.

It seems that the other half of the brain does not think we are worthy of success because it is overwhelmed that it even exists. We are overwhelmed that we were chosen to exist in this massive universe and on this amazing planet and that we understand we exist. It may be overwhelming, it may be all a fluke, but we're here. No one is more special or should strive to be more special than anyone else. We are all equal and worthy and we all deserve joy. It is important to feel worthy and loved by others and by God or the universe.

Most of us want to be kind to others but we may be so insecure that we fear their rejection. Why would that great person be nice back to me? Maybe I'm not worthy. In fact, the only reason she wouldn't be kind back is that she doesn't feel worthy of your love or your acknowledgement.

Life is as simple as acknowledging everyone around you, seeing the good in others, seeing both sides of an issue, being kind and considerate to others, and helping when needed. The opposite will give you negative karma. It takes a bit of work but it really is an ideal system and we should be glad that it is a system where goodness is rewarded and not the other way around.

You have dozens of encounters with other people every day and every encounter is a chance to start a chain reaction to even more happiness. The bus driver, the store clerk, your neighbour, your brother, your sister, your parents, your friends, your teacher, your teammates and your coach all offer you a chance to increase your karma and therefore be happier with yourself. Being happier with yourself causes you to make healthier decisions. Making healthier decisions allows even greater things happen to you and makes you even happier.

While you are getting ready to go to school or work, try not to be concerned about your hair, blemishes on your face and wrinkles in your clothes. Visualize being open and concerned about the others you will encounter today. This does not mean you are neglecting your own needs — quite the contrary. The world will open up for you if you are kind. People will want to be around you. They will want to return the favour of your graciousness and good things will happen to you. All you have to do is smile and give. Give to your friends, family and community and you will be amazed to learn how beautiful and amazing this planet is. You will have all the family, friends, health, spiritual growth and comforts of the Earth you will ever need but you will have earned it. The proof is the results.

# FAQS

## Why is Seeking Power considered Negative?

Many of us think power is a good thing, but it really isn't. Most human problems come from when they want an unfair advantage over another. To have power over a spouse or someone at work, or for a country to have a national policy to be powerful for advantage over another, is always a bad thing because there is no healthy give-and-take. Because of the imbalance, one side will always be resentful and neither side will benefit. A husband who uses financial or physical power over his partner misses out on a healthy relationship and the relationship will eventually fail. The boss who takes advantage of a power position will have employees who won't work to their maximum and will eventually leave. A country that uses power over another will miss out on a healthy trading partnership and will spend more time on disagreements and retaliation. The criminal carries a gun not just for protection but for advantage. The self–centred paedophile is attracted to youth, mainly for the power to control.

Even in business, if you use your powerful position to take advantage of someone, you are really stealing from him.

The mechanic, the banker, the lawyer and all other workers need to be paid fairly but if a powerful position is assumed in order to take advantage of someone else, in the karma realm it is stealing.

We tend to want a position of power when we should be seeking a position of equality and a win-win situation. Countries, companies, relationships, rock bands and sewing clubs will break up if there is no healthy give-and-take.

## Can I Use Thought to Bring Anything to Me?

Two campers are lost on an island for a week. One is going to sit there and wish food to come to him. The other is going to build a trap, go hunting and gathering and work at getting food and building a shelter. Who will be eating first?

It's amazing how positive thinking, praying, visualizing and giving out positive energy can help you achieve goals in life but action requiring energy needs to take place. We have heard of campers that did nothing but hope and pray until rescue came. We forget to factor in the campers that did the same and did not make it.

Everything comes from something. If you imagine yourself driving a brand new Jeep, realize someone has had to design and build it. Why would someone build it and deliver it to you for no reason? If it came to you as a gift from someone, then they had to work for it or build it. It doesn't mean the universe won't open some doors for you and help you pick up some overtime shifts or help you find a quality used Jeep for sale. Even if doors open and you obtain financing to purchase the vehicle, you will still work several years for the exchange of energy to even out the energy that went into building the vehicle. If you are expecting a Jeep to mysteriously drop from the sky onto your driveway, you may be waiting a long time. If you pray for a Jeep to magically come to you, you are asking

God to take it from someone else who has worked for it and give it to you.

You always hear about the lottery winner who prayed or visualized winning and won, but everyone who bought a ticket did that. It was still luck. Go ahead and pray or visualize what you would like out of life. Finally you are focused on something, but understand that what you are really asking for is confidence in the realization that you are worth it and the bravery and determination to tackle your goals. Nothing gets handed to you. Sitting at home doing nothing = nothing in return.

Many successful athletes use visualization to focus on winning a race or event. What they are actually doing is working backwards. An athlete comes up with a goal: "I want to win the gold medal in the hammer throw." Then the brain comes up with what is needed to do this: "I will have to gain 20 pounds of muscle. I will have to hire a nutritionist. I will have to move to get access to better coaching. I have to get my finances in shape so I can concentrate on my sport." Then the process starts and great things happen. His hard work and potential gets him accepted to a university with a great program and coach. He qualifies for some funding and finds a great part-time job that allows for his busy schedule. He trains hard and qualifies and does well at the Olympics. He does not do this by only wishing and dreaming or visualizing it. He must apply energy.

Visualizing, dreaming, wishing or praying can start you on the path to reach your goals, because now you know what you want, but action is needed. We would love to be successful by just imagining success but it comes by taking risks. Only "energy out" will bring you a new job or a new relationship. It takes work to distribute resumes for a job and energy to go out and meet new people. And you will only keep the job or the relationship if you work hard at it.

# SELF-KARMA RATING

Use the Self-Karma Rating to see where you're currently at. Re-do this test in one month and again in one year and see your score grow.

## Health Karma

| | | | | | |
|---|---|---|---|---|---|
| You exercise most days. | 1 | 2 | 3 | 4 | 5 |
| You eat healthily. | 1 | 2 | 3 | 4 | 5 |
| You handle stress well. | 1 | 2 | 3 | 4 | 5 |
| You don't smoke. | 1 | 2 | 3 | 4 | 5 |
| You don't abuse alcohol or drugs. | 1 | 2 | 3 | 4 | 5 |

My health karma is _____/25

## Financial Karma

| You work/study full time. (30 hrs/week or more) | 1 | 2 | 3 | 4 | 5 |
|---|---|---|---|---|---|
| Your job pays well. | 1 | 2 | 3 | 4 | 5 |
| You are well organized/your house is very clean. | 1 | 2 | 3 | 4 | 5 |
| You avoid buying wants (versus needs). | 1 | 2 | 3 | 4 | 5 |
| You don't buy lottery tickets/you know hard work makes you rich, not luck. | 1 | 2 | 3 | 4 | 5 |

My financial karma is_____/30

## Work Karma

| You work at a high energy level. | 1 | 2 | 3 | 4 | 5 |
|---|---|---|---|---|---|
| You are positive to be around. | 1 | 2 | 3 | 4 | 5 |
| You help others/don't mind doing others' work. | 1 | 2 | 3 | 4 | 5 |

My work karma is_____/15

## Social Karma

| You invite others over to socialize. | 1 | 2 | 3 | 4 | 5 |
|---|---|---|---|---|---|
| You are non-judgemental/non-gossiping. | 1 | 2 | 3 | 4 | 5 |

| | | | | | |
|---|---|---|---|---|---|
| You seldom complain/you are fun to be around. | 1 | 2 | 3 | 4 | 5 |
| You take others up on their invitations. | 1 | 2 | 3 | 4 | 5 |
| You initiate conversation. | 1 | 2 | 3 | 4 | 5 |

My social karma is_____/25

## Knowledge Karma

| | | | | | |
|---|---|---|---|---|---|
| You read self-help/information books/magazines/Online forums. | 1 | 2 | 3 | 4 | 5 |
| You discuss new ideas with others and listen. | 1 | 2 | 3 | 4 | 5 |
| You are well educated (college/university/other). | 1 | 2 | 3 | 4 | 5 |

My knowledge karma is_____/15

## Family Karma

| | | | | | |
|---|---|---|---|---|---|
| You take time for family. | 1 | 2 | 3 | 4 | 5 |
| You are open to differences/stay out of drama. | 1 | 2 | 3 | 4 | 5 |
| You seldom yell or argue. | 1 | 2 | 3 | 4 | 5 |
| You like helping family members. | 1 | 2 | 3 | 4 | 5 |

My family karma is_____/20

## General Karma

| | |
|---|---|
| You smile regularly. | 1 2 3 4 5 |
| You give compliments often. | 1 2 3 4 5 |
| You are patient with others. | 1 2 3 4 5 |
| You are positive to be around. | 1 2 3 4 5 |
| You learn from life experiences. | 1 2 3 4 5 |
| You take advice easily. | 1 2 3 4 5 |
| You don't procrastinate. | 1 2 3 4 5 |
| You can think long term but live in the present (you don't worry about the future/you are done with the past). | 1 2 3 4 5 |
| You don't wait for change or action. You make it happen. | 1 2 3 4 5 |

My general karma is_____/45

My total karma is my responsibility. Total karma_____/175

Printed in Canada